CIVIL RIGHTS
IN
FLORIDA

ROBERT REDD

THE
History
PRESS

Published by The History Press
Charleston, SC
www.historypress.com

First published 2023

Manufactured in the United States

ISBN 9781467153225

Library of Congress Control Number: 2023940714

Notice: The information in this book is true and complete to the best of our knowledge. It is offered without guarantee on the part of the author or The History Press. The author and The History Press disclaim all liability in connection with the use of this book.

CONTENTS

ACKNOWLEDGEMENTS

Writing can be a lonely endeavor. At the end of the day, it is the writer and their thoughts, their computer and a stack of books, notes, photocopies, photos, scraps of paper and untold numbers of computer files. It is up to the historian to try to make some semblance of order out of all the materials they have gathered, knowing there is additional source material still out there just waiting to be found and used.

Along the way, the solitary writer will meet up with many individuals who help them, whether it be with encouragement and support, experience or materials. I consider myself fortunate to have befriended many terrific Florida historians who have always offered encouragement and advice. It's a tight-knit group but a welcoming one.

I would like to thank, in alphabetical order, Michael Butler, James C. Clark, Bob Grenier, Michael C. Hardy, Rick Kilby, Joe Knetsch, Rob Mattson and Nick Wynne. My friend Jim Schmidt always deserves thanks for helping me get started on this journey. He patiently walked me through the ins and outs of the proposal process and was instrumental in getting my first book published. I am still eternally grateful. To those I may have forgotten, I apologize. The oversight is completely accidental.

I recently had the opportunity to reconnect with one of my undergraduate professors. Dr. Paul Croce at Stetson University has been full of enthusiasm and encouragement for my work. I think it was gratifying to both of us to see how a struggling undergraduate turned out.

The amazing team at Florida Memory has helped supply many of the images in this book. While the website has its quirks, the humans on the other end do an amazing job, and their contribution cannot be overstated.

University of South Florida special collections librarian Andy Huse went above and beyond to locate material related to Charles Kenzie Steele. The material he provided to my research is much appreciated.

I always like to acknowledge the contributions that local historical societies make to our study of history. Without these dedicated individuals, many times amateur volunteers operating on shoestring budgets, so much local history would be lost. My local friends at the Halifax Historical Society, Ormond Beach Historical Society, Southeast Volusia Historical Society and West Volusia Historical Society are always available when I call or email. They may not have an answer, but I can trust they go overboard to try to find what I am asking about. You, gentle reader, no doubt have similar organizations in your area. Be sure to take advantage of the resources they offer and support them financially when you can.

My friends at Arcadia Publishing are always a source of support and encouragement. Joe Gartrell is always available to listen to my new ideas and provide guidance. He has helped guide me through several books and hopefully will for several more. To my copyeditor, Zoe Ames, thank you. This book would not be what it is without your close attention to detail. It's hard to believe that this is my seventh book (six solo titles and one book with two coauthors).

My mother is always a source of support and encouragement, and it is much appreciated.

It is to my wife, Christina, that I owe the most thanks. She allows me the time and freedom to work on these projects when I need it. She understands the mail delivery of that next "needed" book—and then the fact that it will end up in a pile of other books on the dining room table. I can always count on the knowing roll of the eyes when I tell her the title of the journal article I am reading. She takes it all in stride, and I love her even more for it.

INTRODUCTION

The issues of civil and human rights are never far from the forefront of the news. Those in power, whether elected, appointed or seized, have the ability to impact the lives of each and every person under their authority. It is a staggering amount of trust we put into elected and appointed individuals.

Attempting to understand what these terms mean and do not mean is important.

Cornell Law School discusses civil rights in these terms: "Civil rights refer to legal provisions that stem from notions of equality," adding, that

> *Discrimination occurs when the civil rights of an individual are denied or interfered with because of the individual's membership in a particular group or class. Various jurisdictions have enacted statutes to prevent discrimination based on a person's race, sex, religion, age, previous condition of servitude, physical limitation, national origin, and in some instances sexual orientation.*[1]

Human rights is a much more ambiguous and harder-to-define term. It may mean something different depending on where you are from, your cultural upbringing and, in most cases, your political outlook. The Stanford Encyclopedia of Philosophy states, "Human rights are norms that aspire to protect all people everywhere from severe political, legal, and social abuses." Human rights may include both legal and moral rights.[2]

I have struggled to come up with a strong working definition of what I am getting at in this book. It's not that I don't have opinions on this; it's just that trying to put them into a formal framework can prove difficult. Yes, there are differences between human and civil rights. But should there be? I suppose civil rights (legal) are there to protect human rights (norms)? The reality is that I have still not formulated a written definition I am happy with. The concepts are more complex than what is on the surface when you give them serious consideration. I tend to go with my gut, which asks me, "Is that how I would want a loved one, or myself, to be treated?" If I say no, or hesitate in saying yes, it is probably something that needs to be examined very closely.

In brainstorming for this book and putting together a written proposal, I gathered a listing of possible chapters. These were stories I felt were important and needed to be told in an accessible and time-manageable manner. Some of these stories have been well documented in full-length texts or perhaps in harder-to-find academic, journals while others were not as well known or understood. As might be guessed, the list quickly became unwieldy.

If you browse through my bibliography, you will find information on many stories that unfortunately did not make the final cut for this book, for various reasons. These are incredible stories and ones worth learning more about. Many of these events occurred decades ago. Public schools have limited time, and now limited ability (is this a civil or human rights issue?) to delve into what are important topics. Stories such as those of Rosewood, Groveland and Harry T. Moore are all too often brushed aside in formal education. If it isn't on a standardized test or doesn't help toward a STEM education, the topic is often overlooked. If the topic is considered controversial, teachers may not even legally be able to discuss it, thanks to recent legislation.

The subject of Black beaches is one that academics have published about extensively. Whether it be the general topic or works on individual beaches, the story is important in understanding the concept of "separate but not equal." In Florida, Black beaches such as Virginia Key in Miami and American Beach at Jacksonville have received academic treatments; Bethune Beach in Volusia County and others, while there may be source material about them, have not been covered in this manner.

The founding of New Smyrna in 1768 by Dr. Andrew Turnbull and his partners, on the backs of the labor of slaves and indentured servants, continues to be a difficult story to tell. The story is full of unverified accusations against Turnbull (look, Turnbull was no saint, but much of what is known is only one-sided). While yes, the Minorcans, Greeks and others were legally (civilly) indentured to the moneyed landowners, were they granted and provided with what we would call human rights, such as adequate food, water, clothing and shelter? Were their work conditions safe and humane? Was their indenture time reasonable, and what could they expect once released from their obligation? Were they treated in a dignified manner? These questions raise the issue of presentism and how we today are looking at events of the distant past. Is it fair to examine and perhaps criticize Andrew Turnbull for actions that in the 1760s were normal? To twenty-first-century humans, the idea of indenture is unimaginable. In the eighteenth century, it was accepted. I am not sure there are easy answers here. I do understand that a respected academic is working on a biography of Turnbull. Perhaps, once published, this work will provide deeper insight into the Smyrnea Settlement and what life was like there for those living under indenture.

Nearly sixty years after his assassination, Dr. Martin Luther King Jr. is still as polarizing a figure as he was in the 1960s. Why is that, and how have we as a country not moved past that? Dr. King spent quite a bit of time in Florida, though this is maybe not as well-known as his efforts elsewhere. The subject of his influence in the Sunshine State, in addition to his time in St. Augustine, is ripe for a book-length study.

Claude Pepper and his fight for the rights of the elderly in Florida is a subject that should be of considerable interest to residents of the state. With an aging population and already more than 20 percent of state residents over age sixty-five, Florida is heavily influenced by the wants and needs of the elderly. Do their wants, needs and preferences have the potential to infringe on the rights of those younger than them? Just because you can outvote others does not mean you are right, legally or morally.

Migrant labor is a continuing issue in the state. The State of Florida estimates between 150,000 and 200,000 migrant and seasonal farm workers travel throughout the state as crops ripen. I was unable to determine if this estimate counts only legal residents or includes immigrants working in the United States illegally. Human and civil rights concerns should continue to be strong in this industry. Working and living conditions are human rights concerns, while pay rates are a civil rights concern. A final factor to consider is whether these workers are in the country legally and what impact that has on their employer/employee relationship. Are employees being held hostage, in effect, for fear of their, or their families', deportation? What repercussions are there for landowners who knowingly hire undocumented workers or pay them wages below state and federal mandates?

Ongoing human and civil rights stories continue in Florida. The political focus being placed on, and against, LGBTQ persons in Florida is a prime example, while the political reach, or overreach (depending on your point of view), of untrained politicians into classrooms should give any thinking person reason to step back and reflect seriously on the priorities being shown in Tallahassee. The history of these events is being written now, most often by journalists, whose work will no doubt form the foundations for future full-length books. Future historians writing on these subjects will have to sift through materials as varied as official governmental records, social media posts, YouTube videos, blogs, newspaper articles and editorials, oral histories and published and unpublished memoirs.

I present to you here a selected group of stories that you may or may not be familiar with. Going into this book, I knew of them but was not knowledgeable about them. Perhaps the most widely known of these histories is that of the St. Augustine civil rights protests of 1964. This story has received wide publicity due to a few press photos taken at the time. The story of women's suffrage in Florida is one I might have thought would be easier to track down. There are some good materials available, but it takes some digging to find them. Old newspaper articles are critical to this subject. My coverage cannot be definitive in any way but rather provides an outline of the difficulties faced as women tried to gain the vote. The Tallahassee bus boycott proves that a small but determined group can effect change against an entrenched bureaucracy. The name Roxcy O'Neal Bolton elicits blank stares from most Floridians. Bolton, however, played an outsized role in women's issues in south Florida, even taking on the National Weather Service. And no discussion of civil and human rights in Florida can exclude Jackie Robinson, a man who proved that African American baseball players deserved the opportunity to play at the highest levels. Robinson didn't just break the color barrier in baseball, but in fact, he also served as an inspiration to millions of young children across the country.

While Florida is considered a vacation and retirement paradise, its role in the history of civil and human rights should not be overlooked. Historians of the subject will find much fertile ground to work.

Chapter 1

"FLA. GALS MAY VOTE AT LAST!"

This was the sarcastic headline published on May 16, 1969, in the *Daytona Beach Evening News* after the Florida legislature boldly approved a resolution endorsing the Nineteenth Amendment to the United States Constitution, nearly fifty years after Tennessee became the thirty-sixth state to approve the amendment in a vote on August 18, 1920. The vote by Tennessee legislators provided the three-fourths majority needed for ratification, granting women a guarantee of the right to vote.[3]

Professor Kenneth R. Johnson has proposed that woman suffrage began as a "northern phenomenon. No southerner was associated with the rise of the movement, nor was there any significant suffrage activity in the South until the late nineteenth century." He contends that the southern movement began formally organizing in the 1880s and, by 1913, every southern state had a local suffrage association.[4]

The charge for woman suffrage was fought along two fronts. Both would prove difficult, particularly for those struggling in southern states. The first option open to women was their local state legislatures. Many White male elected officials went about their business believing suffrage was a state's rights issue only.

The second option for those demanding the vote was to pass an amendment to the United States Constitution. This was also to prove a daunting task, requiring a two-thirds vote in both houses of Congress and then approval by the legislatures of three-fourths of the states. This would again prove a monumental task, with many legislators suspicious of the need for such an amendment. The National American Woman Suffrage Association (NAWSA) took advantage of both options.[5]

The Wyoming territorial legislature granted women the right to vote and hold office on December 10, 1869, a right that continued after the territory achieved statehood in 1890. Shortly after, the territories of Utah, Washington and Montana granted suffrage to women. In 1893, Colorado became the first full-fledged state to approve woman suffrage. Nearly twenty years later, in 1910, the woman suffrage movement was empowered by approval in Washington State. The 1912 party platform for the Progressive Party—or the Bull Moose Party, as it is often called—under Theodore Roosevelt included support for woman suffrage as part of the "Square Deal."[6]

When Ella C. Chamberlain attended a suffrage conference in Des Moines, Iowa, in 1892, a fire was lit in her, and she determined then to fight for woman suffrage in her home state of Florida. Later, after returning to Tampa, she was offered the opportunity to write a newspaper column with topics geared toward women and children. Chamberlain was ready to jump on this opportunity to promote equal suffrage, and her reply to the proposal was, "The world was not suffering for another cake recipe and the children seemed to be getting along better than the women."[7] Despite her apparently contrary nature, Chamberlain was still allowed to pen her column.

The following year, 1893, saw Chamberlain elected president of the newly formed Florida Woman Suffrage Association, a group associated with Susan B. Anthony and the National American Woman Suffrage Association. Later that year, she represented the Florida branch in the national meeting held in Washington, D.C.[8]

Growth of this organization in Florida was slow. Fundraising was always an issue. Pamphlets needed printing; dues to the national organization required payment; travel for officers and other expenses were a constant. Fundraisers like the December 1894 bazaar, which raised $125, helped keep the organization active.[9]

In 1895, the Florida Woman Suffrage Association met in Tampa. By then, membership had increased to approximately one hundred. Chamberlain was reelected president, Emma Tebbitts of Crescent City and Jessie M. Bartlett of St. Petersburg were elected co–vice presidents, Nellie Glenn of Melrose was named secretary and J.L. Cae of Limona became treasurer. Only Tebbitts, arguably, did not live in the Tampa area, perhaps showing that the movement had not gained traction throughout the entire state.[10]

Perhaps the most famous suffragette, Susan B. Anthony spent her life in the fight for equal voting rights for women. With Elizabeth Cady Stanton, she formed the National Woman Suffrage Association. In 1872, Anthony was arrested for voting and fined one hundred dollars. Anthony died in 1906, fourteen years before the passage of the Nineteenth Amendment guaranteeing women the right to vote. *Image courtesy Library of Congress.*

It was also in 1895 when *Woman's Journal* asked "why southern women desire the ballot." In words shocking today, Chamberlain answered in part,

> *I contend that Southern women, more than those of any other section of our country, need the authority of the ballot. Intelligent, educated and deeply religious, the Southern woman finds herself dominated by the lowest class of voters. Laying aside the humiliation of being governed by the ex-slave, who is just emerging from centuries of barbarism and servitude, consider his unfitness as a voter. Ignorant, thriftless, and too often vicious and depraved, his vote as easily purchased as his lightest possession, his is the natural prey of conscienceless politicians, and stands before the Southern woman a constant menace to her already restricted liberties. And this large body of degraded and undesirable Southern voters is being augmented by large numbers of foreigners, immediately adopted into the body politic by the easy law which manufactures American citizens out of rejected foreign material, on the simple declaration of intention.*
>
> *I am a free-born American woman. My ancestors left their bloody footprints on the snows of Valley Forge, and were among the brave Kentucky riflemen, the immortal few who gave their lives at the battle of New Orleans, for liberty for themselves and their children. I deny that my brother American can properly represent me. How, then, can I, with the blood of heroes in my heart, and the free and independent spirit they bequeathed me, quietly submit to representation by the alien and the negro?*[11]

Chamberlain's concern over African American voting, and the desire for woman suffrage, is one that would be voiced many times, and not just in Florida. As early as 1867, abolitionist Henry Blackwell from Massachusetts advocated for allowing women to vote to negate the votes of the newly freed slaves. Giving women the vote was promoted in order to maintain white supremacy.[12]

Others advancing the cause of woman suffrage as a counter to Black voters included NAWSA president Anna Howard Shaw, who was quoted as saying, "Never before have men made former slaves the political masters of their former mistresses." The Woman's Christian Temperance Union (WCTU) waged a two-pronged attack. The WCTU promoted woman suffrage not just to "settle the race question in politics" but also because, "since alcoholism was a vice more common to men and had a detrimental effect on the home, temperance advocates felt that women's votes would result in the passage of anti-liquor laws."[13]

The woman suffrage movement in Florida was growing until the departure of Ella C. Chamberlain in 1897. When Chamberlain left Florida, a leadership vacuum arose. As historian A. Elizabeth Taylor succinctly wrote in 1957, "Mrs. Chamberlain and her followers had endeavored to sow the seeds of feminist thought in Florida but had failed to establish any enduring organization there." The woman suffrage movement in Florida would remain dormant until 1912.[14]

The early years of the twentieth century were fruitful for the movement, and it gained popularity and momentum nationally. In June 1912, the Florida movement blossomed in Jacksonville with the creation of the Florida Equal Franchise League (FEFL). Under the leadership of presidents Katherine Livingston Eagan and Roselle C. Cooley, the organization grew to forty-five members. Despite joining the National American Woman Suffrage Association, the Jacksonville members failed to expand outside of their locale.[15]

The movement began to spread, and local groups arose throughout the state, but there was no centralized leadership. In April 1913, a small group met in Orlando to discuss ways to unite. This led to a November 1913 convention, also held in Orlando. Out of the November meeting, the Florida Equal Suffrage Association was born, with Mary Safford elected state president.[16]

The creation of the state organization allowed the holding of regular conferences. These were often single-day events and were held in growing communities such as Pensacola, Miami, Daytona Beach and Tampa. Regular actions included run-of-the-mill business such as officer elections and event planning and coordination. Occasionally, a nationally known speaker might be in attendance.[17]

Despite woman suffrage being a rather progressive issue, that is not always how activists saw themselves. As we have seen, the suffrage issue was seen by some as a way to offset Black votes. Pensacola members during the 1910s were later described by the League of Women Voters as follows:

The traditions of the South were part of the culture of these women. They were interested in enfranchisement but were afraid—not of themselves, not of the public and not of ridicule. They were afraid of aligning themselves with a movement at odds with their ethics. They were conservative women who held the standards of womanhood high. They believed a woman's first duty was to her child and that, above all things, a woman should love the home and being a homemaker. They opposed the force of violence and would not be a part of a militant movement.[18]

The members of the Pensacola Equal Suffrage League were quite active and petitioned regularly for speakers and organizers from the NAWSA. In March 1914, Lavinia Engle, the NAWSA field secretary, arrived in Pensacola for a two-week visit that included a whirlwind of meetings and speaking engagements. In her March 13, 1914 speech at the San Carlos Hotel, Engle reinforced the anti-militant view that local women had of themselves. "American women do not want militancy—we leave that for the English suffragettes. There is a great difference in the suffragist and the suffragette. The American women do not believe in the militant methods any more than do the American men."[19]

When asked "What would you do with the vote of the colored woman?," Engle answered in a manner that the likes of Ella C. Chamberlain, only thirty years prior, might have recoiled at.

> *Well, the vote of the colored man has not disintegrated the political life of the South, why should that of the southern woman?…But, if the Negro woman should vote, it might be that their vote would be as much value as that of many men. For the heart of the mother is the same, in the breast of every woman, and these women, these mothers of the country, who are asking for the vote, are fighting for their children. And if the Negro women fight for their children, and make of them better citizens, it might yet be that even their vote should become a power for good.[20]*

Speakers from out of state were becoming more commonplace as attempts to gain supporters for woman suffrage, both female and male, intensified not just in Florida but also across the country. These speakers visited many cities throughout Florida, spreading the word in an attempt to increase support and thus put pressure on politicians.

Louisianan Kate Gordon and Washington state congressman J.W. Bryan visited Florida in 1914. During a stop in Jacksonville, Gordon asked those in attendance, "Has woman the right to express her opinion? Then what is the ballot but an expression of opinion.…Would you deny woman a weapon with which to defend herself? Then what is the ballot but a weapon of defense." Speaking in agreement with Gordon, Congressman Bryan added, "The only true democracy is a democracy that really extends equal rights to all and special privileges to none, and that can come only when woman and man together cast the ballot and together assist in making the laws that shall govern them both by the consent of both."[21]

Pattie R. Jacobs of Alabama was a frequent Florida speaker, including at statewide conferences in 1914 and 1917. In November 1917, during the height of the Great War, Jacobs spoke in Tampa. She proposed that suffrage be considered a war measure:

> *Some state that the woman's place is in the home and yet the war is thrusting them into fields they never occupied before. Economic conditions forced a woman to seek her livelihood. It was not from choice but necessity. We agree that woman's place is the home, but not in the home. We regard the world as the home, and we want the ballot to protect the home.*[22]

Anna Howard Shaw, the past president of NAWSA, toured Florida many times throughout the decade, visiting cities such as Tampa, Winter Haven, Miami, Jacksonville and Orlando. Local newspaper accounts show her to have been enthusiastically received, with the *Miami Herald* calling her "one of the greatest women America has produced." She infused her speeches with a mix of humor, seriousness and solemnity as she orated on not just suffrage but also the growing international crisis known as the Great War, or World War I.[23]

Speaking on behalf of the federal woman suffrage amendment, Tennessee resident Anne Dudley spoke throughout Florida, reminding listeners of the support suffrage was receiving from President Woodrow Wilson. When Dudley was questioned about the issue of states' rights, she was quick with a reply both showing her southern tendencies and addressing what she considered the more important issue: "I believe in state rights, too, when they do not conflict with human rights, but has it ever occurred to you that men never stop to think of state rights in relation to anything but suffrage."[24]

Despite growing memberships and considerable public support, organizations campaigning for woman suffrage were always fighting a battle to stay afloat financially. Membership dues were usually nominal, most often fifty cents per year or less. Other revenue sources were required. Taking a cue from religious revivals and churches, suffrage groups took public speeches and gatherings as an opportune time to "pass the plate." The 1914 Jacksonville speeches given by Kate Gordon and J.W. Bryan raised $120. The widow of noted politician William Jennings Bryan helped raise over $650 when she hosted a silver tea in Miami. A series of fundraising conferences were held in 1919 and raised over $1,500 in total donations.[25]

Two competing factions were striving to push forth woman suffrage: the National American Woman Suffrage Association and the National Woman's Party. These two organizations highlighted the two possible ways for women to achieve the vote—the first option being amendments to state constitutions (states' rights), which was the preferred action of the NAWSA, while the National Woman's Party worked exclusively toward achieving its goals on the federal level. It is, of course, too simplistic to state that NAWSA was only interested in achieving the vote on a state-by-state basis, as it did exert pressure at the national level as well.

The National Woman's Party was considered to be the more militant of the two organizations. Its members were more willing to take a direct and vocal route, agitating lawmakers directly at times. Led by Alice Paul, the group failed to take a firm grip in Florida. As we have seen, most women in Florida disapproved of the militant route.

While the National Woman's Party was never the major player in Florida, the group did have a presence. In May 1917, Alice Paul and Ella St. Clair Thompson of North Carolina, visited Florida to help set up a state branch. At a meeting in Jacksonville, they achieved this goal, with Hannah Detwiller being named chair.[26]

Militant actions were still considered by most Florida women to be unbecoming and against their cause. Some women, such as seventy-three-year-old Mary O. Nolan of Jacksonville, did not believe that way and were prepared to fight for what they believed were their rights. During the late afternoon of November 10, 1917, Nolan and forty other women were arrested as they lined up outside the gates of the White House in hopes that President Woodrow Wilson would see their plight. The press reported the event was quite orderly. Policemen quickly gathered the women and led them to six waiting patrol wagons. The women were swiftly escorted to a local courthouse where they were each released on twenty-five dollars' bond. The women were said to have "[gone] to the patrols with a smile and no resistance almost at once after they had taken their places flanking the entrances."[27] For her actions, Nolan received a jail sentence of

Seventy-three-year-old Mary A. Nolan of Jacksonville joined the National Woman's Party in 1917. That November, she was arrested while protesting for the vote in Washington, D.C. She received a sentence of six days. Undeterred, Nolan would be arrested several more times while protesting for woman suffrage. *Image courtesy Library of Congress.*

six days. Others participating in the march received sentences varying from thirty days to six months.[28]

Women arrested while advocating for the cause of suffrage were to use their imprisonment as a sort of badge of honor. A group of twenty-six women who had served sentences for their activities related to suffrage toured the country, using their imprisonment as a call to other women to join the cause. The group arrived in Jacksonville by rail in February 1919, where they were met by Helen Hunt, then chair of the Florida branch of the National Woman's Party. They held an afternoon rally at Hemming Park and an evening meeting at the Morocco Temple, a building designed by noted Jacksonville architect John Klutho, then home to the Jacksonville Shriners.

During the evening meeting, twelve of the twenty-six women dressed in prison garb to help further illustrate their plight. Several of the women were quoted in the local newspaper regarding their confinement. New York City resident Mrs. H.O. Havemeyer told those in attendance, "It is no fun to go to jail. It takes courage to go to jail and face such conditions." Lucy Burns said, "We did it all for democracy and we get mockery," adding that she and other suffragists had been treated badly while behind bars. The National Woman's Party meeting ended with the passing of a resolution calling on President Woodrow Wilson to urge passage of a constitutional amendment guaranteeing woman suffrage.[29]

Women were continuing to organize and seeking ways to exert pressure on politicians. During the September 1918 Florida Equal Suffrage Association meeting, held in Daytona Beach, those in attendance passed a resolution in support of granting women the right to serve on school boards.

> *Whereas, President Wilson, the world's leader of democratic principles, has appealed personally and publicly to the leaders in the government of the United States to give to women their rightful place in America, and, Whereas, the educational development of the youth of the country is largely under the supervision of women, and in view of the fact that many of our United States have already given to women school suffrage,*
>
> *Resolved, that we, the citizens of the state of Florida in attendance at the public meeting on September 18th, 1918, at Daytona, go on record as pledging our support to a measure to be introduced at the extra session of legislature, Tallahassee, granting to the women of Florida the legal right to serve on school boards, thus placing Florida in the front ranks in the educational world.[30]*

Daytona Beach women continued to show growing interest in the suffrage movement during 1918. On November 20, a local branch of the Florida Equal Suffrage Association was formed. With the state organization present, Mrs. C.G. Hendricks was elected branch president, with Dr. Josie M. Rogers named secretary and treasurer.[31] Only two nights later, in the city, Justina Wilson, recording secretary of the National Woman Suffrage Association, gave a talk to the Florida Federation of Women's Clubs. The local paper quoted the *Baltimore Star* in describing her as "an alert, up-to-the-minute woman of keen mentality and profound thought. In person she is attractive and impelling."[32]

As we have seen, for the men and women fighting for woman suffrage, there were two routes to accomplish their goal. Both were daunting, most often through legislatures dominated by conservative White men.

In 1913, the issue of woman suffrage received its first serious consideration in the Florida legislature. Palm Beach representative H.L. Bussey put forth a resolution calling for the immediate enfranchisement of women by amending the state constitution. On April 25, 1913, a public hearing was held, with supporters, including Jeanette Rankin, on hand to provide encouragement. The resolution was passed along to the full house without a recommendation.

When the bill came forward to the full house, Representative Bussey stated he did not favor woman suffrage and had only introduced the legislation at the request of the West Palm Beach Branch of the Federation of Women's Clubs. He further stated that if the proposal passed the legislature and went to the people for a vote, he would vote against it.

Others in the Florida legislature were strongly opposed to woman suffrage as well, with several men willing to go on record publicly with their views. Duval County representative St. Elmo W. Acosta and H. Clay Stanford of Osceola County both claimed that woman suffrage was a northern ideal that the South wanted no part of. Hernando county representative L.C. O'Neal harkened to what he considered traditional values, stating that woman suffrage was "contrary to tradition, history, manners, modesty, and the best thought of the country." He continued with the old trope that if "women were granted the ballot they would be lowered from the exalted position which they now hold." Putting forth both sexist and racist views, John M. Gornto of Lafayette County claimed that if women were given the vote, it would "bring on marital unhappiness, divorces, and a disruptive domestic condition" and that giving the vote to African American women would "entail such a train of evils that it would be impossible to conceive of what

"Suffragists led the way" is the theme for this 1963 photo taken in Tallahassee, re-creating a 1913 protest in favor of woman suffrage. *Image courtesy State Archives of Florida; Ellis Finch, photographer.*

might follow."[33] With attitudes such as these, it is no wonder that any attempt to pass equal suffrage legislation in Florida was doomed.

The suffragists were hardly in a mood to concede, and when the state legislature reconvened in 1915, those in favor of voting equality were there. Despite setbacks in both the house and the senate, a small victory was achieved. On April 29, 1915, the state legislature approved incorporation of the city of Fellsmere, in what is now Indian River County. This incorporation included equal suffrage for women.[34]

To this day, Fellsmere claims to be the "Birthplace for Equal Suffrage for Women in Florida." In 2004, the National Organization for Women of Indian River County and the Florida Department of State erected a historic maker with the following text:

> *"The population of Fellsmere is of a high type of intelligence, with lofty ideals and wise execution. Progressive in all things, perhaps no better indication of the fact may be given than the unanimous vote of the town granting unrestricted suffrage to women."* Fellsmere Tribune, *March 8, 1916.*
>
> *At a February 1915 meeting at the Dixie Theater, Fellsmere citizens accepted the articles of incorporation unanimously. The charter included a unique proposal that women be "granted full and equal privilege for suffrage in municipal elections." Local bills seldom received close scrutiny from legislators, and the equal suffrage provision went unnoticed. In signing the act that created the town of Fellsmere, Governor Park Trammell, in effect, gave women the right to vote in its municipal elections. In the June 19, 1915 city election, Mrs. Zena M. Dreier was the first woman to cast a ballot in Fellsmere, in all of Florida, and south of the Mason-Dixon Line. The town residents took much pride in this unique woman's right, and urged neighboring municipalities to follow the "Fellsmere Way" to equal suffrage. In 1919, a U.S. Constitutional amendment granted suffrage to women. But history will note that Fellsmere led the way.*[35]

In 1917, the issue of suffrage was again at the forefront as state legislators came to session. Early in the session, the senate heard from Mary Elizabeth Bryan, who explained to senators that women could be both wives and voters. She stated that not only would suffrage provide dignity to women, but it would also offer additional common interests for husband and wife. On April 20, the senate brought the amendment to a vote. While the amendment had gained popularity and passed with a majority vote of eighteen for and eight

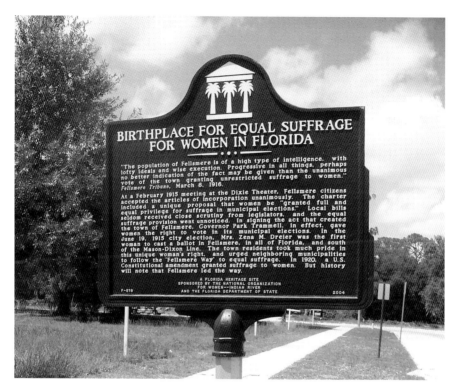

Fellsmere, Florida, a community of around five thousand people in Indian River County, lays claim to being the "Birthplace of Equal Suffrage for Women in Florida." In 2004, the Indian River County branch of the National Organization of Women sponsored this historic marker, located along County Road 507. *Image courtesy Wikimedia Commons.*

against, the amendment did not receive the required three-fifths votes of the total senate needed for approval. It appeared the amendment was dead a third time, until the legislature took up the bill again on the twenty-third, this time passing it twenty-three to seven. With no debate, the amendment was sent to the Florida house.

Over the next several days, the Florida House of Representatives held a spirited debate on the merits of woman suffrage. Future Florida governor David Sholtz of Volusia County came out in favor of women receiving the vote, making the claim that men already respected ladies and giving them the vote would not change this viewpoint. Hamilton County representative C.A. Stephens believed women should leave politics to the men (no doubt meaning White men), claiming, "Divine law placed man at the head of the family and made him the ruler and governing power of nations." The vote of forty for and twenty-seven against suffrage fell short of the needed three-fifths majority required, and equal suffrage failed for a third time at the state level. Despite this setback, communities such as Pass-a-Grille, Palm Beach and Moore Haven were authorized and included the vote for women. Progress was slow, but it was being made.[36]

During a special session of the state legislature in late 1918, efforts were made to persuade state politicians to encourage Florida representatives in Washington, D.C., to pass the proposed "Susan B. Anthony Amendment." While the measure failed, communities such as Orange City, Daytona Beach and DeLand had local bills passed granting suffrage to women.[37]

In the spring of 1919, the United States Congress acted toward ratification of the Nineteenth Amendment to the Constitution. On May 21, the House passed the amendment by an overwhelming 304–90. The Senate, however, was slower to react and took until June 4 to narrowly pass the amendment 66–30. It would now be up to state legislators to pass the amendment.

Four members of the House represented Florida during the 1919 vote. Members Herbert Drane and William Sears voted for approval, while John H. Smithwich and Frank Clark voted against the amendment. In the Senate, both Florida members, Duncan U. Fletcher and Park Trammell, voted against the amendment. Fletcher claimed that the issue should be decided at the state level and not through the federal government. He went further, however, perhaps getting to the real reason behind his views. Fletcher believed that the Fifteenth Amendment (which guarantees African American men the right to vote) was enacted in error and that allowing women, including an estimated two million African American women, the right to vote would only be compounding a prior mistake.

Park Trammell further voiced the racist attitudes so prevalent in Florida at the time:

> *In our state at present our elections are participated in almost exclusively by our white men and the negro is not a factor in the selection of our public officials. I am opposed to any proposition which would possibly invite greater and more extensive participation in our election on the part of the negro population. I am also opposed to any policy that may invite and probably stimulate citizens of other states who do not understand and appreciate our race problem in making an effort to bring the negroes of Florida into politics.*[38]

Timing for Florida state elected officials could not have been better. The amendment was sent to states while the legislature was still in session,

Herbert Jackson Drane was a Democrat from Florida who served in several elected positions, including eight terms in the United States House of Representatives. In 1919, Drane was one of two Florida representatives to vote in favor of the Nineteenth Amendment to the United States Constitution. *Image courtesy State Archives of Florida.*

and they had the opportunity to be the first to ratify the new amendment. Governor Sidney Johnston Catts urged the legislature to act quickly. As it had in the past, the Florida legislature failed to act, throwing away the opportunity to take a leadership role on the issue. While blame was passed around, it appears that the final reason was that leadership could not ensure the votes needed for passage.[39]

States throughout the country were ratifying the suffrage amendment, and by the end of March 1920, only two states were still needed. When Washington ratified the amendment, that left only one state ratification needed before women would be guaranteed the right to vote. On August 26, 1920, the Tennessee legislature, by the narrowest of margins, passed the Nineteenth Amendment, and when Secretary of State Bainbridge Colby certified and signed the amendment, it became an official part of the constitution and the law of the land.[40]

On the morning of September 7, 1920, women across Florida began lining up to register to vote. In Duval County, Helen Hunt was the first to register. In Escambia County, women were allowed to register beginning on

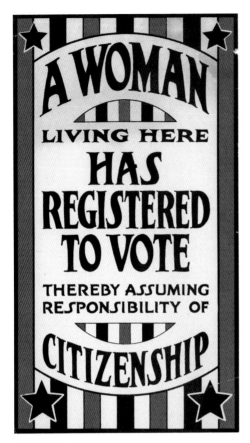

Left: On August 26, 1920, Tennessee became the thirty-sixth state to approve the Nineteenth Amendment. On September 7, 1920, Florida women began to register to vote, assuming the responsibility of citizenship. Window signs such as this served a dual role: they showed that a voting woman lived in the residence but also encouraged other women to register to vote. *Image courtesy Smithsonian National Museum of American History.*

Below: Maxine Baker served in the Florida House of Representatives from 1963 to 1972. Baker was active in the League of Women Voters and served on Governor LeRoy Collins's Special Constitutional Advisory Committee in the late 1950s. Baker may be best remembered for the 1972 Florida Mental Health Act, more commonly known as the Baker Act. *Image courtesy Florida Memory; David Fountain, photographer.*

September 8, when seventy-eight women registered. On that same day in Escambia County, Isabella Ingraham took the office of deputy supervisor of registration and helped register these women to vote.[41]

Did women use their newly won rights? The results of the 1920 elections in Florida show a mixed bag. During the 1916 race for governor, nearly 81,000 ballots were cast, while in 1920, the same race attracted just shy of 133,000 votes. The presidential election of 1916 drew 83,000 votes, while the 1920 election garnered 156,000. Although these increases may seem significant, approximately 227,000 Florida women were guaranteed the right to vote. Nationally, while 68 percent of eligible males voted, only one-third of eligible women voted in 1920, certainly not the success that suffragists had hoped for in the years leading up to the passage of the Nineteenth Amendment.[42]

While Florida had the opportunity to be the first state to ratify the Nineteenth Amendment, political leaders failed to seize the opportunity put before them. Not only did they fail to take a leadership role, but they also let the issue lie until 1969, when the Florida League of Women Voters requested the state take action as the fiftieth anniversary of passage approached. Both houses unanimously passed Resolution 1172, finally acknowledging a woman's right to vote. Maxine Baker, a Democrat from Miami, stated, "I feel the enlightened Legislature of 1969 would like to rectify an oversight of 50 years ago."[43]

Chapter 2

"WELL, THIS IS IT"

Jackie Robinson Breaks the Color Barrier

For years, a small contingent of sports writers and newspapers had been asking, "What's wrong with baseball?" Heywood Broun of the *New York World-Telegram*; Alvin Moses and others at the *Pittsburg Courier*, a newspaper geared toward an African American readership; and Jimmy Powers at the *New York Daily News* were aggressive in questioning the motives and rationale that kept quality Black baseball players from playing in the major league.

Broun went so far as to bring up the topic publicly during the February 1933 annual dinner of the New York Baseball Writers Association. Broun asked why Black athletes were good enough to compete in college sports, at the Olympics and in professional football but not at the highest level of baseball.[44]

Historian Chris Lamb, in his exhaustive work on Jackie Robinson's 1946 spring training, drives home the point that this story is about more than baseball: "The story of Jackie Robinson's first spring training captures America as it moved, or staggered, toward its promise of equal rights for all. In addition, the drama of baseball's first integrated spring training dramatizes the way in which the issues of integration, segregation, and civil rights were covered by the nation's black press as well as its white mainstream press."[45] In perhaps a simpler way of looking at it, Jackie Robinson embodied the hopes, dreams and aspirations of millions of African Americans in a time when they had shown their bravery and loyalty during World War II but were returning to a country little different than they had left.

There were no African Americans in organized baseball. By "organized" baseball, White executives meant the major leagues and their associated

In a short career of only ten seasons, Jackie Robinson shattered not only the color barrier in Major League Baseball but also the belief that African Americans were not good enough to play in "organized" baseball. Robinson was elected to the Baseball Hall of Fame in 1962, receiving 77.5 percent of eligible ballots. *Image courtesy Smithsonian National Portrait Gallery.*

minor league teams. The Negro leagues, amateur teams, international leagues and others were not deemed worthy of the label. Despite having no African American players and exhibiting no interest in such, team owners, league leadership and the mainstream White press perpetuated the myth that baseball was open to African American players. In 1941, writing for the *Sporting News*, J.G. Taylor Spink voiced the opinion that "no matter how humble the home from which an American youth may come, an opportunity to rise above his environment is open to him if he has the necessary energy and talent. That is the American way, and baseball, as America's national pastime, offers an easy entry into the field of opportunity."[46]

In a 1942 interview, Major League Baseball commissioner Kennesaw Mountain Landis claimed, "There is no rule, formal or informal, no understanding, subterranean or otherwise....If Durocher, or any other manager, or all of them, want to sign one, or twenty-five, Negro players, it's all right with me." In response to this, New York Yankees president Larry MacPhail put forth five reasons there were no Blacks in baseball. First, he

Kennesaw Mountain Landis (*right, with New York City mayor James Hylan*) served as commissioner of Major League Baseball from 1920 to 1944. One of Landis's first acts as commissioner was to deal with the 1919 Black Sox Scandal and enact rules dealing with gambling and throwing games. *Image courtesy Library of Congress.*

claimed, there was no demand for Black players. He then claimed that there were no Black players who could earn a spot on a major league team. His third excuse was that integration would ruin the Negro leagues. He further claimed that Black players did not wish to play in organized baseball. His final reason blew up the prior statement of Landis: he claimed that baseball had an agreement forbidding management to sign Black players.[47]

As we will see, MacPhail's claims, with perhaps the exception of the third and fifth, were false. Black fans turned out in larger-than-anticipated numbers to see Jackie Robinson, and others, play. Robinson proved to his teammates, managers, the press and the public that Black players had the talent to play at the highest levels of baseball. While the signing of Robinson—and other top stars of the Negro leagues—did have an adverse impact on this level of baseball, the impact for the players, the sport and the nation was positive. In breaking the color barrier, Jackie Robinson opened opportunities for players across the league. MacPhail's statement that Black players did not wish to play in organized baseball was clearly false. Athletes are natural competitors and wish to match their skills against the best out there. For Black baseball players, this was no different. In organized baseball, they were also able to earn a better living to help support their families. In addition, Robinson realized that what he was doing had a larger societal impact than just playing baseball. Finally, there may not have been a written agreement barring the signing of Black players, but there can be little doubt that there was a gentleman's agreement to continue segregation.

Despite this gentleman's agreement, Branch Rickey, president of the Brooklyn Dodgers, began making plans that would rock the world of organized baseball. In 1945, he had been secretly scouting, looking for the right Black player or players to sign. By "the right player," he meant several things. The first was, of course, ability. There were many highly qualified players who were toiling for Negro league teams. Rickey's second criterion was the harder to fulfill. He needed a player who would not lash out against whatever racism he might encounter from fans, teammates or the press.

Robinson was an army veteran, having been drafted into service in 1942. Despite an arrest for refusing to sit at the back of a transport bus in 1944, a charge of which he was acquitted, Robinson served honorably and received an honorable discharge in November 1944. In 1945, Robinson began playing for the Kansas City Monarchs, a Negro league team that featured the legendary Satchel Paige, himself a future major league player and 1971 inductee into the Baseball Hall of Fame, as one of his teammates.

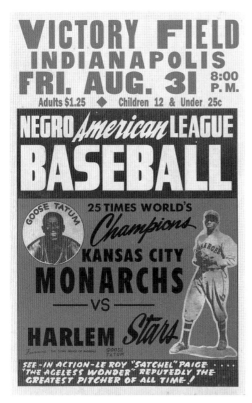

Left: LeRoy "Satchel" Paige was a teammate of Jackie Robinson on the 1945 Kansas City Monarchs Negro league team. Paige has been considered by many experts one of the greatest pitchers of all time despite not playing in the majors until age forty-two. Paige was elected to the Baseball Hall of Fame in 1971. *Image courtesy Smithsonian National Museum of African American History and Culture.*

Below: In a long professional baseball career, Branch Rickey's most lasting achievement was the signing of Jackie Robinson to a contract with the Montreal Royals for the 1946 season and allowing Robinson the chance to play with the Brooklyn Dodgers the following year. Rickey (*right*) was elected to the Baseball Hall of Fame in 1967. *Image courtesy State Archives of Florida.*

Robinson was clearly the star on the Monarchs team. He hit .375 and had an on-base percentage of .449. He was exhibiting the potential of a major league player, and Branch Rickey knew it.

In August 1945, Rickey met with Jackie Robinson to discuss a potential contract. Young Robinson's talent was not in doubt. Rickey had to be assured of his temperament, however. Could he handle the taunts and insults from fans and opposing players? Could he bite his lip and not fight back against the racism that Rickey feared might show? How would his family, including his new wife, Rachel, stand up under these stresses? Once Rickey was assured that Robinson was the right man, the two quickly struck a deal, and in August 1945, a landmark contract was signed. Jackie Robinson was signed to the Montreal Royals of the Triple A International League, a step below the major leagues. Only the world was not to find out for several months.[48]

When his deal was announced publicly on October 23, 1945, Robinson; Hector Racine, the Royals' president; and Branch Rickey Jr., head of the Brooklyn Dodgers minor league system, faced a questioning press. The young ball player told them, "I realize what I'm getting myself into, I also realize how much it means to me, my race, and baseball."[49]

Branch Ricky Jr., in discussing the signing, added, "Jack Robinson is a fine type of young man, intelligent and college bred, and I think he can make it, too." When discussing the issue of race, Rickey Jr. added that some players may "steer away from a club with Negro players on its roster. Some of them who are with us now may even quit, but they'll be back in baseball after they work a year or two in a cotton mill."[50]

Hector Racine praised Robinson to the press, calling him "a good ballplayer" and the signing a "point of fairness," stating that Black athletes had earned the right to compete against Whites. Racine cautioned, however, that Robinson would be competing for his spot on the roster during spring training, to be held in Daytona Beach. The *Sporting News* quoted Robinson as saying, "Guess I am just a guinea pig in this noble experiment."[51]

Press reaction to the signing was mixed, as might have been expected. The Black press exploded. The *Chicago Defender* stated that this was an opportunity not just for Jackie Robinson but also for all Black citizens. Writing for the paper, Fay Young added, "[This is] a step toward a broader spirit of democracy in baseball and will do much to promote a friendlier feeling between the races." The *New York Age*, assessing Robinson's prospects, proclaimed, "Knowing that he will have to be Superman will bring out the best in him; and the best in him should prove sufficient to break up another myth that Negroes do not belong in white baseball."[52]

The *Pittsburgh Currier*, long a proponent of allowing Black players into Major League Baseball, called this action "the most democratic step baseball has made in 25 years.…This is a movement that cannot be stopped by anyone. They may be able to detain it for a while, but not for too long. The world is moving on and they will move with it, whether they like it or not." In this article, Robinson followed up on his guinea pig reference, stating he would be "the best guinea pig that ever lived, both on the field and off."[53]

In talking with the *Baltimore Afro-American*, Robinson poured out his feelings and the pressures he was under. "I feel sort of as if everyone was looking at me. I feel that if I flop, or conduct myself badly—on or off the field—that I'll set the advancement back a hundred years. Why, I feel that all the little colored kids playing sandlot baseball have their professional futures wrapped up somehow in me."[54]

Black civic leaders understood the importance of Jackie Robinson signing this contract and were quick to comment. Adam Clayton Powell Jr., then a young first-term member of the House of Representatives representing the Harlem neighborhood of New York City, stated, "This is a definite step toward winning the peace, and now that this gentleman is in the International League, the other leagues will not be able to furnish any alibis." Roy Wilkins, the future executive director of the National Association for the Advancement of Colored People, added that this signing meant Blacks "should have their own rights, should have jobs, decent homes and education, freedom from insult, and equality of opportunity to achieve."[55] While the ideals espoused by Powell and Wilkins were noble, they were premature, as we know.

White, or "mainstream," press greeted Jackie Robinson's signing with mixed emotions. The *New York World-Telegram* accused Rickey of having ulterior motives, believing that the signing was politically motivated and not based on any skills Robinson might have had. *New York Daily News* columnist Jimmy Powers called Robinson a thousand-to-one shot at making it in White baseball.[56]

In his in-depth examination of the national press reaction to the Jackie Robinson signing, historian Chris Lamb noted that magazines such as *Life*, *Time* and *Newsweek* failed in their obligation to understand the magnitude of the story. Yes, they reported on Robinson signing with the Royals, but they failed to follow up on the larger story of not just integration in baseball but also the opportunity this created across the county for Black citizens in all walks of life, not just sports.[57]

During his examination, Lamb reviewed coverage in the leading sports newspaper, the *Sporting News*. In its November 1, 1945, article titled "Montreal

Roy Wilkins served in many positions during his tenure with the NAACP, including editor of the *Crisis*, executive secretary and executive director. While often at odds with various civil rights organizations, Wilkins was awarded the Presidential Medal of Freedom in 1969 by President Lyndon B. Johnson. *Image courtesy Library of Congress; Carl Van Vechten, photographer.*

Puts Negro Player on Spot," the paper lashed out, accusing Rickey of touching "off a powder keg in the South, unstinted praise in Negro circles, and a northern conviction that the racial problem in baseball is as far from a satisfactory solution as ever." The *News* then accused Rickey of placating politicians in his signing of Robinson as an attempt to sidestep a New York law known as the "Anti-Discrimination Law. This has to do, in part, with the barring of Negroes from jobs and professions." In analyzing Robinson's prospects, the same editorial stated, "Robinson conceivably will discover that as a 26-year-old shortstop just off the sandlots, the waters of competition in the International League will flood far over his head. One year ago, with baseball suffering from manpower stringencies, Robinson would have faced a better chance on the technical side of the game." The editor closed by clearly missing the importance of the occasion: "The Sporting News believes that the attention which the signing of Robinson elicited in the press around the country was out of proportion to the actual vitality of the story."[58]

Reporter Al Parsley, in the same issue of *Sporting News*, played into race baiting in a way unfathomable in mainstream press today. Parsley stated, "This Robinson is definitely dark. His color is of the hue of ebony, by no means can he ever be called a brown bomber or a chocolate soldier, even though he did serve four years in Uncle Sam's Army."[59]

Despite the role the city would play in upcoming events, the Daytona Beach newspaper was oddly silent on the signing, running several Associated Press articles that had been distributed nationally. There was no local input or opinion in the articles.[60]

Ahead of the town playing a role in the Jackie Robinson story, the *DeLand Sun News* announced the signing on page 6 with a United Press stock story highlighting segregationist laws in Daytona Beach. Daytona Beach city manager James M. Titus was quoted: "We have a very good situation between the races here, because we give the Negroes everything we give the whites. There is no discrimination but there is segregation. Negro teams play in our main park, but we have never had mixed teams." The article went on to state, "Officials of the hotel at which the Montreal club will stay had no comment to make, other than to point out that only whites may register there."[61]

Jackie and Rachel Robinson had a difficult time just getting to spring training in February 1946. They arrived safely in New Orleans but were bumped from their next flight, allegedly due to military priorities. They were then able to fly to Pensacola where, again, they were bumped; a White couple was given their seats. They found transport on a Greyhound bus, seated in the back, in seats reserved for Negroes. Years later, Robinson recalled the events and his feelings: "I had a bad few seconds, deciding whether I could continue to endure this humiliation. After we had been bumped a second time at the Pensacola Airport, I had been ready to explode with rage, but I knew that the result would mean newspaper headlines about an ugly racial incident….I could have blown the whole major league bit."[62] Rachel recalled the miserable bus ride: "I looked at my new going-away trousseau suit and the ermine coat that Jack had saved for years to buy me as a wedding gift, and I could see the stains from the overalls worn by the men going to work in the fields and the rock quarries. I felt like weeping."[63]

On arrival, Robinson found a mixed grouping at camp. Branch Rickey had signed a second Black player, twenty-seven-year-old right-hand pitcher Johnny Wright, who had played for the Homestead Grays of the Negro leagues. Wright had also played baseball while serving in the navy. By all accounts, Wright was a good pitcher with a lively fastball. Some even considered him to be a better prospect than Robinson.[64]

Awaiting Robinson and Wright was manager Clay Hopper, a native of Mississippi, who struggled with the prospect of coaching Black players. When asked about having Black players on his team, Hopper is alleged to have said, "My father is dead. If he were alive he would probably kill me for managing a black player." Hopper was to learn much during the season, and Robinson later said that the manager had treated him fairly.[65]

The Montreal Royals began spring training in Sanford, then a rural community perhaps best known at the time for growing celery. The population was around eleven thousand. When spring training officially opened on March 4, 1946, Robinson, Wright and close to two hundred White players were competing for jobs on the two Dodgers AAA teams.

As he walked toward the field to begin his training, Robinson said to Bob Finch, an assistant to Branch Rickey, "Well, this is it." The first day of camp was uneventful. Robinson participated in running, stretching and batting practice. Robinson took swings off "Iron Mike," a pitching machine that allowed batters to face major league–speed pitching without wearing out live arms. There were conflicting stories about Robinson's success, but he was quoted as saying, "I felt as happy as a youngster showing off in front of some other boys." He closed out the day with press interviews. In discussing the differences between White baseball and playing in the Negro leagues, Robinson explained, "You fellows who have been around the big leagues all the time don't appreciate what good coaching and teaching means. Fellows like us on the sandlots just have to learn the best we know how. But maybe, it'll be different. I hope so."[66]

The peace did not last long, however. After the second day of practice, Black sportswriters Wendell Smith and Billy Rowe, who were covering the emerging story, received a visit from an unknown White man with a message to get Robinson and Wright out of town or there would be trouble. Once he heard this unsettling news, Rickey quickly pulled the two ballplayers to the comparative safety of Daytona Beach.[67]

While nobody knew what the reaction would be in segregated Daytona Beach, Rickey was not going to give up. City manager James Titus commented that the players would be welcome in the beach community. For his part, Rickey made sure to reiterate that the players and the Dodgers were not trying to challenge local segregation ordinances but rather trying to build the best baseball teams they could.[68]

Although Daytona Beach did not display the hostility found in Sanford, segregation was in full force. In 1946, there was legal segregation. Black residents were mandated to live in one of two areas: north from Volusia Avenue (now known as International Speedway Boulevard) to North Street or south from Volusia Avenue to Shady Place. The Florida East Coast Railway tracks to the east and Nova Road to the west were additional barricades. These artificial barriers were put in place "in order to promote the public peace, welfare, harmony, and good order."[69]

As had been planned previously, the Montreal Royals moved their training camp to Daytona Beach. Robinson and Wright were not allowed to live with their teammates at the Riviera Hotel but rather were forced to find accommodation with residents. Jackie and Rachel Robinson roomed with Joe and Duff Harris, while Johnny Wright stayed at the home of Vernon Smith.[70]

While the Harrises and Smith did the best they could, this separation from their teammates was difficult for Robinson and Wright. Team sport athletes

THE RIVIERA — ON THE HALIFAX — NEAR DAYTONA BEACH, FLA.

FLORIDA'S FOREMOST ALL YEAR HOTEL WITH COTTAGES

During the 1946 Brooklyn Dodgers spring training in Daytona Beach, Florida, White players received accommodations at the luxurious Riviera Hotel, while Jackie Robinson and Johnny Wright were forced to find rooms with local African American families due to segregation laws in the city. *Image courtesy the author.*

understand the need to build friendship, trust, cooperation and loyalty. While this can be accomplished on the field, those hours off-field are crucial. That is when players truly get to know and understand each other. Riding the bus to and from practice, sharing communal meals, playing cards and other games and telling tall tales about back home allowed these friendships to form, trust to be won and loyalty to develop. Enforced segregation robbed Robinson and Wright, along with their White teammates, of these opportunities.

Each day, the White players rode the bus from the Riviera Hotel to Kelly Field, near the campus of Bethune Cookman College (now Bethune Cookman University). Robinson and Wright walked to practice each day. The players took part in drills and scrimmages. The inexperience of both Black players showed, as they went at full speed from the beginning. The coaches tried to dial them back in an attempt to prevent injury.

Robinson was considered a good prospect, but the Dodgers had multiple quality shortstops, and his arm was always considered suspect for the position. He tried to make up for this perceived deficiency by throwing as hard as he could during his time in the field. As the coaches feared, his arm reacted negatively to the strain. After the second day, he reported to the press that his arm was sore. Indeed, the following day, he was unable to make throws from the shortstop position to first base. Coach Hopper shut him down, allowing him to take batting practice and reporting his condition to Rickey.

On hearing of Robinson's ailment, Rickey immediately went to Kelly Field. He told Robinson he had to participate even if hurt. "Under ordinary circumstances, it would be all right, but you're not here under ordinary circumstances. You can't afford to miss a single day. They'll say your dogging it, that you are pretending your arm is sore." Recalling the incident years later, Robinson stated, "I couldn't throw. On top of that, I couldn't hit. The harder I tried, the more I popped up or pounded the ball into the dirt....The more I tried, the more tense I became."[71]

His sore arm, however, became an unintended blessing. The long throw from the shortstop position to first base was going to be a problem for Robinson even if he was healthy. The decision was made to move him to second base. While the throw was shorter, the position required a whole new set of skills, skills that Robinson did not have at the time. He approached the position change with a positive attitude, stating, "If the manager wants me at second base, that's where I'll play. I'm here to make good."[72]

The new second baseman received plenty of advice. Rickey and Hall of Famer George Sisler, then a coach for the Dodgers, worked closely with Robinson. Hitting coach Paul Chervinko gave Robinson plenty of attention, helping him with technique and to understand tendencies in a new league. This perceived extra coaching was not lost on players or the press, with one writer penning, "It's do-gooders like Rickey that hurt the Negro because they try to force inferior Negros on whites and then everybody loses. Take this guy Robinson. If he was white, they'd have booted him out of this camp long ago."

Despite comments such as this, Robinson was to receive assistance in learning his new position from an unlikely source: Lou Rochelli, the man assumed to be the starting second baseman. As Robinson was to recall,

A young and talented player, Lou Rochelli, had been—until my arrival—the number-one candidate for second base. When I got the assignment, it would have been only human for him to resent it. And he had every right to assume that perhaps I had been assigned to second base instead of him because I was black and because Mr. Rickey had staked so much on my success. Lou was intelligent and he was a thoroughbred. He recognized that I had more experience with the left side of the infield than the right, and he spent considerable time helping me, giving me tips on technique. He taught me how to pivot on a double play. Working this pivot as a shortstop, I had

George Sisler (*left, with fellow Baseball Hall of Fame members Babe Ruth, center, and Ty Cobb*) spent many hours working with young Jackie Robinson on his approach to hitting. Sisler was himself a career .340 hitter who was elected to the Baseball Hall of Fame in 1939. *Image courtesy Library of Congress.*

> *been accustomed to maneuvering toward first. Now it was a matter of going*
> *away from first to get the throw, stepping on the bag, and then making the*
> *complete pivot for the throw to first. It's not an easy play to make, especially*
> *when the runner coming down from first is trying to take you out of the play.*
> *Rochelli taught me the tricks, especially how to hurdle the runner. I learned*
> *readily, and from the beginning, my fielding was never in question.*[73]

Lou Rochelli, who prior to spring training had only five major league games to his credit, would never play in the majors again. He bounced around the Brooklyn farm system until 1956, spending most of his seasons playing part time for lower-level minor league teams. Rochelli passed away on October 23, 1992, at the age of seventy-three in Victoria, Texas.[74]

As spring training progressed for Robinson and his Royals teammates, games were rapidly approaching. The Royals had twenty-six games scheduled, ample time for prospective players to show their abilities in hopes of securing one of the limited, and cherished, roster spots. The young second baseman was still nursing a sore arm, and when the Royals opened games against the St. Paul Saints, a second Triple A–level Dodger farm team, Robinson found himself on the bench resting. He continued to take batting practice; however, his sore arm impacted his swing, and he continued to feel the pressure building on him.[75]

Finally, on Sunday, March 17, Jackie Robinson was listed on the starting lineup card. That day, the Royals were scheduled to challenge Brooklyn at City Island Ballpark. City Island looked much different in those days in comparison to the modern view. City Island was, well, an island, as opposed to what modern construction has accomplished, including the creation of much "land" that is home to several government buildings and ample parking.

That Sunday, the hopes and dreams not just of Jackie and Rachel Robinson and Branch Rickey but also of millions of Black Americans would be fulfilled. Robinson's teammates understood in some capacity. One teammate told him, "All you have to do is make a good showing against the Dodgers and you'll be sure of staying with Montreal."[76]

Robinson was, of course, not so sure of this. The Royals and Dodgers were not confident in how Robinson would be treated by fans, and it was not a given that Daytona Beach would allow the game to proceed with Black

City Island, Recreation Center, Daytona Beach, Fla.

Originally opened during the 1910s, City Island Ball Park was renamed Jackie Robinson Ball Park in 1989, with a large formal ceremony to follow in 1990. The facility was added to the National Register of Historic Places in 1998. *Image courtesy the author.*

and White players together. Robinson recalled the situation years later: "The grapevine had it that I would not be allowed to play; that the authorities had been putting terrific pressure on Mr. Rickey. What I didn't know was that the shoe was on the other foot. The Dodger boss was the one exerting the pressure. He had done a fantastic job of persuading, bullying, lecturing, and pulling strings behind the scenes."[77]

When game time arrived, the stadium was packed. Despite the enforced segregation, more than four thousand attended the game; one thousand in attendance were Black. One person who was not in attendance was Branch Rickey. Rickey held strict views regarding the Sunday Sabbath and would not bend, even for what was going to be a landmark event, not just in baseball but also for American society.[78]

As the Royals came to bat in the top of the second inning, Robinson patiently waited his turn to bat, sure he would be booed and heckled by the majority-White crowd. Of course, there was a smattering of boobirds, but what he heard shocked him. He heard cheers and applause. This sound was not just from the Jim Crow seats along the right field line but from White fans, as well. In writing later, Robinson recalled one fan saying, "Come on, Black boy! You can make the grade," and another yelling, "They're giving you a chance—now come on and do something about it." Hardly enlightened words in modern society, but in the South of 1946, this was positive encouragement.[79]

On Monday, the *Daytona Beach Evening News* ran coverage on page 10 under the headline "Walker's Bat Ices Dodgers' Win; Robinson Plays." On Robinson, the paper reported,

> *All eyes were focused upon Jackie Robinson, hefty Montreal second sacker and the first negro to appear in an organized baseball game. Playing under terrific pressure, Robinson conducted himself well afield during his five-inning stint. He handled two chances aptly.*
>
> *At bat Robinson popped out in the second and fourth frames. The ex-Army lieutenant slammed a hard-hit grounder in the sixth and was safe when Howie Schultz was forced at second. Robinson stole second, drawing a wide round of applause from the audience. Catcher Ferrell Anderson singled to short center and Robinson, running like a scared rabbit, breezed across home plate with the Royals' second and final run of the afternoon.*[80]

Newspapers in Sanford and DeLand did not cover the event. Other Florida papers ran brief national AP or UPI stories. Dodgers manager Leo

Happy Chandler served as the second commissioner of Major League Baseball from 1945 to 1951. He would also serve as governor of Kentucky for two separate terms and serve one term in the United States Senate. Chandler was elected to the Baseball Hall of Fame in 1982. *Image courtesy Library of Congress.*

Durocher was complimentary: "Although Robinson didn't get a hit today, he looked like a real ballplayer out there. Don't forget he was under terrific pressure. He was cast in the middle of a situation that neither he nor the fans had ever experienced before. But he came through it like a champion. He's a ballplayer."[81]

Press reports of the treatment the Black prospects were receiving was generally positive in the days after Jackie Robinson's debut. In an interview with the *Pittsburgh Currier*, Major League Baseball commissioner Happy Chandler commented on the treatment Black players could expect if they made the Royals team: "I think they'll be treated all right. As far as I can detect, no one seems resentful about them being on the team at this time, and I can't see why anything should crop up later on. You can never tell, but I think they'll be treated all right." Others reported "absolutely no friction" and similar assessments.[82]

Despite positive press reports, things were not always calm in the Royals camp. Roster spots were at a premium, and there was concern that Robinson, and perhaps Wright, would earn spots based on their race rather than ability. Johnny Jorgensen stated that you didn't "hug them or kiss them or anything like that"; you went about your business, "you just observed them, talked to them, played catch. Hell, I didn't think anything about it. But some of the southern boys were a little concerned. I didn't have time to worry about

[Robinson]. I was worried enough about myself."[83] Jorgensen would break through to the Dodgers team in 1947 and have a five-year major league career, primarily as a platoon third baseman.[84]

While Robinson's arm was still suspect and his hitting had not come around as anticipated, there was tremendous interest in him. This interest came from a Mexican league scout by the name of Robert Janis. The Mexican league had anecdotally offered Bob Feller $300,000 to sign for three years, an offer Feller denied receiving. Janis made a stab to sign Robinson, introducing himself to the player at Kelly Field by offering him a $6,000 one-year contract plus expenses for player and wife. Robinson flatly refused the offer, telling the scout, "I am not interested. There is too much at stake." When Janis showed up at City Island Ballpark later in the day, he was banned from the premises by Branch Rickey himself.[85]

While Daytona Beach had allowed Jackie Robinson to play without incident, the same could not be said for other communities in the state. The *New York Post* commented that "Branch Rickey knew he was handling a hot potato when he signed Jackie Robinson and Johnny Wright. But the potato is really getting hot now and fans all over the country are waiting to see how far Rickey will go to defend the presence of his colored performers." By calling Robinson and Wright "performers" rather than athletes, columnist Leonard Cohen tipped his hand that racist journalism knew no geographic bounds.[86]

The Royals were to take on the Jersey City Giants on Sunday, March 24, in Jacksonville. The *Florida Times-Union* made much out of the possibility of a Black man playing with Whites at Durkee Field. On Friday, however, the paper announced the game was canceled because the field was "not available." The field was not available due to the actions of Jacksonville Parks and Public Property director George Robinson who decided to enforce local laws prohibiting integrated sporting events: "Rules, regulations, and policies of the Jacksonville Playground and Recreation Board, prohibit mixed contestants in athletic events."[87]

Jacksonville was not the only city to ban integrated baseball. The Royals were scheduled to take on the Indianapolis Indians, a Dodgers AA team, in DeLand on March 25. Fumbling over themselves for an excuse, DeLand authorities claimed the game had to be canceled because there was to be a night game on the twenty-sixth and in order for that game to proceed, the field lights had to be tested, which included digging up cabling in the field of play. On March 28, a second game in Jacksonville was canceled despite the Royals having made the bus trip from Daytona Beach and a large number of disappointed fans already at the stadium.[88]

This cancellation did several things. First, it hardened the resolve of Branch Rickey. Prior, he had stated the view that the Dodgers would obey segregation ordinances. They were not trying to force integration on cities. After the disrespect shown his team and players, Rickey decided if Robinson and Wright were not welcome, the Royals would not play. Mel Jones, general manager for the Montreal Royals, was quoted in the *Afro-American* as saying, "We don't care if we fail to play another single exhibition game."[89]

The second impact from the canceled game was a large press backlash against the city. Wendell Smith, wrote in the *Pittsburgh Currier* of Jacksonville, "It is a city festering from political graft and vice. And as a result there is less progress there economically, politically, and racially than any other city of a comparable size below the Mason-Dixon line." The *Chicago Defender* piled on: "If Montreal had left the Negro players behind, the setback would have encouraged the obstructionists to close the gates tight against any additional dark aspirants. Montreal has accepted the Negro players and is determined that they be used in all contests according to their ability to play rather than their skin color. They proved this in Jacksonville." Chevy Chase Presbyterian Church in Washington, D.C., in a letter printed in the *Washington Afro-American*, wrote, "Democracy cannot be real so long as its members discriminate against each other. We feel that you have done a great injury to democracy and to brotherhood."[90]

An additional outcome from the missed game in Jacksonville was the realization for Robinson and Wright that there was a fountain of support for their efforts. Robinson, writing about the large number of fans wishing to see the Jacksonville game, said, "That meant a lot to us. It meant that it wasn't the people of Jacksonville who objected to our playing in the park—it was the politicians. Had the decision been left to those people in line, the game would have been played."[91]

While his arm strength was still in question, Robinson started to hit as March turned to April. The hits became more regular, and Jackie was learning to utilize his speed, laying down bunt singles and also stealing bases. Branch Rickey was quoted in the *Pittsburgh Currier*: "He'll hit. The only question is his arm. I only hope it comes around."[92]

Despite the confidence shown in Robinson, there were more questions regarding Johnny Wright, as the pitcher continued to struggle. The *Brooklyn Eagle* quoted Rickey as saying about Wright, "He's 28 years old and the Royals have 12 pitchers. If Wright can't make the Montreal staff, he will be released." Already close to alone, Robinson faced the prospect of losing his closest teammate.[93]

It was well known there were many high-level prospects toiling for little money and even less fame in the unorganized Negro leagues. Branch Rickey, already having raided talent in Robinson and Wright, was not finished. On April 4, 1946, Rickey announced the signing of catcher Roy Campanella from the Baltimore Elite Giants and pitcher Don Newcombe from the Newark Bears and their assignment to the AA Nashua team of the New England League. Both would be excellent major league players, with Campanella earning election to the Baseball Hall of Fame. Newcombe won more than 150 games in a twelve-year career, interrupted by service during the Korean War.

When the Royals announced that both Robinson and Wright had earned roster spots, a collective sigh of relief came from Rickey, the players, the Black press and Black fans across the country.[94] Wendell Smith wrote in the *Pittsburgh Currier*, "After six weeks of tedious training, Jackie Robinson and Johnny Wright have won berths on the Montreal Royals baseball club. They are now officially a part of Organized Baseball—a distinction no Negro player has had since way back in the eighties."[95]

Now that they were on the team, both men had to continue to work hard in order to keep their spot. Roster spots were not guaranteed. The pressure of spring training would not lessen after heading north for the regular season. Wendell Smith continued his impressive coverage of the story, writing, "Never in history have two ballplayers had so many people pulling for them to make good, but at the same time, never in history have two ball players been so dependent upon those same fans who are pulling for them, for they could very easily make or break Montreal's Robinson and Wright."[96]

Robinson was quoted in the *Pittsburgh Currier* on this pressure, saying, "I started swinging at bad balls and doing a lot of things I wouldn't have done under ordinary circumstances. I wanted to get a hit for them [the Black fans] because they were pulling so hard for me."[97]

Jackie Robinson reacted well to the pressure and rewarded Branch Rickey and the millions of fans, Black and White, following his story. In his first official game, taking on the Jersey City Giants, Robinson had four hits in five at bats, scored four runs and stole a base. It was a great start in what was to become a banner year.[98]

For the full 1946 season, Robinson put up incredible statistics. He played in 124 games and tallied 155 base hits. He had a batting average of .349 and an on-base percentage of .468. He stole forty bases and was only caught stealing fifteen times. He had set the table for his debut with the Brooklyn Dodgers the following year.[99]

On April 15, 1947, Jackie Robinson played in his first regular season Major League Baseball game. He would go on to win Rookie of the Year that season, batting .297 and scoring 125 runs. *Image courtesy Smithsonian National Museum of African American History and Culture.*

As for Johnny Wright, his season did not go well. He only appeared in two games before being released. The control problems that plagued his spring training never subsided. He returned to the Negro leagues, where he finished the season and played again in 1947.[100]

When Jackie Robinson broke the major league color barrier in 1947, he did so with a splash, winning Rookie of the Year and finishing fifth in the Most Valuable Player voting, with a .297 batting average and 175 hits. His career took off from there. In a ten-year career, he would be named an All Star six times, was named Most Valuable Player once and received MVP votes eight times. His career batting average was .313, and he had more than 1,500 hits. The Dodgers played in six World Series while Robinson was on the team, winning once in 1955.[101]

In today's world of analytics, advanced scouting and every year a new statistic for fans to understand, Robinson's career statistics might not earn him Hall of Fame consideration. However, Jackie Robinson's impact went beyond what he accomplished statistically on the field. In 1962, the Baseball Writers Association of America elected Robinson to the Baseball Hall of Fame with 77.5 percent of the vote. In 1997, Major League Baseball retired Robinson's number, 42, making this the first number to be retired league-wide. Beginning in 2007, with a request from Ken Griffey Jr. and with the blessing of the Robinson family, players were allowed to wear the commemorative number on April 15 each year, a day designated as Jackie Robinson Day.

The city of Daytona Beach continues to show its pride for the role it played in helping to integrate baseball. In 1989, City Island Ballpark, the field where Jackie Robinson played his first game against major league talent, received a new name: Jackie Robinson Ballpark. First opened in the 1910s and expanded with grandstands in 1929, it is said to be the oldest stadium being used in minor league baseball.[102] The field has been in almost continual use for minor league baseball in the Florida State League, serving as spring training headquarters for the Montreal Expos and as home to the Bethune Cookman University Wildcats baseball team.

On September 15, 1990, City Island Ballpark was officially christened Jackie Robinson Ballpark in a grand ceremony featuring dignitaries such as Jackie's widow, Rachel Robinson. Rachel recalled those difficult days during 1946: "I went to the ballpark every day. In the stands, I sensed a lot of what he was experiencing. I heard from others here that I would enjoy shopping at the downtown stores…that because of the goodwill from Mrs. Bethune [Dr. Mary McLeod Bethune] Daytona Beach merchants welcomed blacks into their stores."[103]

Part of the renaming celebration included the dedication of a large sculpture of Robinson "standing with two small boys, one black and one white. Robinson wears a Montreal Royals uniform, the Dodger farm team he played for while here." The sculpture is the work of artist Jules LaSalle, a sculptor based in Montreal who created the original on which the Daytona statue is based. LaSalle made minor adjustments to the original casting to make the Robinson figure even truer to life. LaSalle stated that creating the Daytona image it was a "great pleasure and honor. People here were ready to respect the project and idea." Rachel Robinson gushed over the work: "I love the statue. It captures his [Jackie Robinson's] essence. It inspires everyone who sees it. You can't just walk by it without being affected by it. And every time I see it, I'm reminded how very much Jack cared about children."[104]

Perhaps more than any other individual, Dr. Mary McLeod Bethune served as a positive influence on race relations in Daytona Beach. The respect she garnered allowed African Americans, such as Rachel Robinson, to be able to shop in downtown stores. *Image courtesy Library of Congress.*

In the years since Robinson's passing, he has received many accolades and attempts to acknowledge the wrongs of the past. In 1997, Major League Baseball retired Robinson's number, 42, from future use, with future Hall of Fame pitcher Mariano Rivera grandfathered in as the last player allowed to wear the number. Rivera retired in 2013, and since then, no player has been allowed to regularly wear the number 42. In 2007, Major League Baseball designated April 15 Jackie Robinson Day. This date was selected due to it being opening day in 1947, Robinson's first in the major leagues. On April 15, 2009, a tradition began: all players, managers and coaches wear the retired number in honor of Robinson and his contributions to the game of baseball.

Over the years, the City of Sanford has acknowledged the mistakes and injustices inflicted by Sanford police chief Roy G. Williams when Jackie Robinson attempted to play in the city in 1946. In 1997, then city commissioner Whitey Eckstein said, "It was a bad thing. We shouldn't have done it. We need to make it right with the Jackie Robinson family."[105]

While it took several years, the City of Sanford did make the considerable move to strip Williams's name from the park where Robinson attempted to play baseball. During its August 10, 2020 meeting, the city commission unanimously passed Resolution 2889 "dismissing the name of 'Roy G. Williams Park' and restoring the name of 'Elliot Avenue Park.'"[106]

In the memorandum attached to the resolution, the city makes the strange assertion that "although the park has been referred to as 'Roy G. Williams Park' there is no evidence that the city actually designated that name." The memorandum continues, "This proposal is to dismiss the name of the park as 'Roy G. Williams Park' by means of adopting a resolution to the extent that the park has improvidently been referred to as a park named after him. Further, the park's name 'Elliott Avenue Park' would be acknowledged and restored as it is clear that the City would not want to have a park named after Mr. Williams."[107]

On October 23, 2022, the City of Daytona Beach and the State of Florida unveiled a state historic marker honoring Jackie Robinson, Johnny Wright and Kelly Field at the newly renamed Julia T. and Charles W. Cherry, Sr. Cultural and Education Center.

Chapter 3

"WE WOULD RATHER WALK IN DIGNITY THAN RIDE IN HUMILIATION"

These words, attributed to Reverend Charles Kenzie (C.K.) Steele (and also spoken by Dr. Martin Luther King Jr. in the wake of the Montgomery bus boycott), became a galvanizing call for participants in the Tallahassee bus boycott of 1956.[108] In the 1950s, despite being the state capital of Florida, Tallahassee was still a comparatively small town. Even though it boasted both Florida State University and Florida A&M University, the total population in 1950 was only 27,237, of which 9,373, or approximately 35 percent, were African American.[109]

As they were everywhere in the South of the 1950s, race relations were, at best, complicated in Tallahassee. Writing for the Anti-Defamation League of B'nai B'rith, authors Charles U. Smith and Lewis M. Killian discuss what they have called the myth of the "Golden Age of Racial Harmony" that existed before May 17, 1954.[110] On this date, the United States Supreme Court handed down its landmark decision on the case of *Brown v. Board of Education*. The Brown case overturned the standard set in *Plessy v. Ferguson* of "separate but equal," finding:

> *We conclude that, in the field of public education, the doctrine of "separate but equal" has no place. Separate educational facilities are inherently unequal. Therefore, we hold that the plaintiffs and others similarly situated for whom the actions have been brought are, by reason of the segregation complained of, deprived of the equal protection of the laws guaranteed*

Thurgood Marshall cut an imposing figure in front of, and later behind, the bench. Marshall argued on behalf of the NAACP in front of the United States Supreme Court in numerous cases, winning the large majority. He served as counsel during *Brown v. Board of Education*, a case that ultimately threw out the "separate but equal" doctrine. Marshall would be appointed to the United States Supreme Court in 1967 by President Lyndon B. Johnson. *Images courtesy Library of Congress.*

by the Fourteenth Amendment. This disposition makes unnecessary any discussion whether such segregation also violates the Due Process Clause of the Fourteenth Amendment.[111]

The myth of the "golden age of racial harmony" was one often spread by locally elected officials in an attempt to mask the realities in their communities. In the years prior to *Brown*, southern whites often spoke of having good race relations in their communities. White leaders were under a misguided belief that African Americans were content in their position, and African Americans were often seen as being well off, despite most having fewer educational, professional and personal opportunities than White residents. Outside agitators (e.g., the NAACP) and the Supreme Court were often seen as the root of racial problems. Local racism was not considered the problem.

Mid-twentieth-century Tallahassee did display a mixed message in some respects when it came to race. Make no mistake, racism and segregation were the norm—often, the legal norm. One local ordinance forbid what was called fraternization. The issue of fraternization went further under the state's board of control. The Florida Board of Control was tasked with creating rules and guidelines for public universities in the state. The board of control was replaced in 1965 with the Florida Board of Regents.

In Tallahassee, one of the rules created by the board of control involved fraternization between students at the White Florida State University and African American students at Florida A&M University. Students from the two universities were prohibited from attending social gatherings together, and Florida State students were not to set foot on the Florida A&M campus unless accompanied by a parent.[112]

Despite this wall of segregation, Florida A&M did play an important role in the community in the eyes of many White people. Shopkeepers welcomed A&M students and their parents—or at least their money. It was accepted that faculty from the university were better off than the average Black citizen, and in general, they were treated with a higher level of respect. The Florida A&M band and bands from local African American high schools were always allowed to perform in parades and special events.[113]

In civic matters, the issue of segregation was readily apparent. Tallahassee had a separate municipal swimming pool. In a show of just how segregated the community was, the city spent money to create a separate golf course for African Americans. The Black community did not have access to a large public auditorium space. While the Tallahassee police department did employ two African American officers, they were limited to patrolling Black areas of the community.[114]

Authors Smith and Killian have made an interesting observation regarding Tallahassee, African Americans and the revival of the Ku Klux Klan during the years after World War II. African Americans were able to register to vote and carry out that duty, although they did so in lower percentages than White residents. It was during these years that the Florida head of the Ku Klux Klan lived in Tallahassee. Despite this and the fact that meetings were regularly held locally, no terrorist attacks were reported in the city. Why this was, Smith and Killian do not theorize. Perhaps it was due to the city being the state capital and potential attackers' fear of local lawmakers. Maybe the proximity of Florida A&M University and a potentially active group of students, faculty and staff played a part. Perhaps the Klan felt that Black residents of Tallahassee "knew their place" and there was no need for violence.[115]

It is due to these reasons that Smith and Killian write, "Viewed through the glass wall of segregation, Negroes in Tallahassee no doubt appeared contented and relatively well-off in the eyes of the whites." The "golden age of racial harmony" was at work in Tallahassee. The glass wall was to come crashing down during the summer of 1956.[116]

When Florida A&M students Wilhelmina Jakes and Carrie Patterson boarded a public bus in Tallahassee on May 26, 1956, they did so without the goal of starting a major civil rights movement. In less than a week, actions taken that day led students and residents to begin a protest that would shake the ground on which locals of both races lived.

On Saturday, May 26, 1956, three students from Florida A&M University stepped onto a city bus, bound for the downtown shopping district. The three young women paid their dime fare and searched for seating. The back of the bus, reserved for African American riders, was crowded that day. One of the three students took a place standing near the rear of the bus. The other two students, Wilhelmina Jakes and Carrie Patterson, sat in two open seats next to a White woman on a bench directly behind the bus driver.[117] This small action by Jakes and Patterson was the spark that inadvertently started the Tallahassee bus boycott. As Charles Kenzie Steele stated in a speech given that October, the city was to find out that "old Tallahassee is not what she used to be."[118]

Max Coggins, the Cities Transit bus driver that day, looked in his mirror before pulling away and was jolted by the sight of two African American students sitting next to a White woman at the front of the bus. Jakes recalled the incident in 1981:

> When we sat down, the driver said, "You girls can't sit there." I said, "Why?" He said, "You just can't sit there." I got up, went to him and said, "Give me back my dime and I will get off." He said, "I can't give you your dime." I returned to my seat and I sat. He drove the bus to the nearest service station; he went into the station and made a call. He returned to the bus and parked and said, "Everyone remain seated." Within five minutes three cars loaded with policemen came. Two of the officers came on the bus. They talked with the driver and then came over to Carrie and I. One of the officers said, "Are you girls having a problem?" I explained to him what had happened and told him that I would get off if the driver would give me my dime. He then said, "You girls want a ride—then I'll give you a ride; come with me." So, Carrie and I, we followed the officer to his car and got in. He took us to the police station. When we got there it appeared as if the entire police force was there to greet us. It was somewhat frightening. He charged us for inciting a riot.[119]

At the police station, the young women were provided with a single phone call. News of the arrest eventually reached Edna Calhoun, the dean of women at Florida A&M. Calhoun contacted Moses G. Miles, the dean of students, who arranged with a bail bondsman for the release of the young students. Bail for not moving to the rear of the bus was twenty-five dollars each. The women were released to the custody of Miles.

News of the arrests spread quickly throughout the community. They were front-page news the following day. Not only did the local press run with the story, but others learned of the arrests, as well. Robert Saunders and Charles Kenzie (C.K.) Steele, both officials in the National Association for the Advancement of Colored People (NAACP) were alerted when a reporter contacted Saunders regarding the arrests. Saunders pushed the issue up the ranks, contacting Roy Wilkins, the executive director of the NAACP.[120]

Saunders and Steele visited the students at their home, expressing support for their actions but providing no formal plan for a reply, let alone for a bus boycott. Despite what on the surface could have been considered a minor incident, the *Tallahassee Democrat* decided it appropriate to print the off-campus address of the two students. In the late afternoon of May 27, the women were alerted to a burning cross on their lawn. Friends and school officials evacuated Jakes and Patterson to the safety of the university campus.[121] The days of the "golden age of racial harmony" in Tallahassee went up in flames that evening.

Tallahassee had been a "weak Civil Rights town" prior to the arrest of Jakes and Patterson.[122] Local white officials, the NAACP and most local Black leaders underestimated the resolve of African Americans living in Tallahassee. The unintended actions of two young students—neither of whom were members of the NAACP or, for that matter, any organized civil rights group—helped spark something in residents: a need to fight back, even if not physically; a desire for basic human respect and dignity; and a desire to be treated on an equal basis with White citizens.[123]

It was not just racist White residents who became aware of the incident. Students at Florida A&M had learned of the arrest, and that Sunday, they made plans for a campus-wide protest on Monday, May 28. Led by student government president Broadus Hartley, hundreds of students gathered in Lee Hall to hear Hartley recount the actions of the prior days. This story, along with students' personal experience of how African Americans were often treated by White bus drivers, led them to act. "They did not want to be humiliated anymore."[124] It was at this meeting, with no outside agitators and no pressure from the NAACP or big-city power brokers, that the students alone decided to boycott city buses for the remainder of the semester.[125]

When the city buses came through campus, students boarded the buses and asked Black riders to support the boycott and get off the bus. Black riders, despite generating 60 to 70 percent of the city's bus traffic, were accustomed to poor treatment and verbal abuse. With limited exceptions, the students' urgings were met with success. The boycott had officially begun.[126]

As word of the boycott spread, the local White community showed a lack of understanding of the issue and the resolve of local Black residents. On Tuesday, May 29, an editorial in the local newspaper incorrectly and condescendingly theorized that Jakes and Patterson "may have been impelled by a misunderstanding of what the United States Supreme Court rules was their right in intrastate bus seating."[127] The case that the *Tallahassee Democrat* referenced is that of *Flemming v. South Carolina Electric and Gas Company*. Here, the court affirmed an appellate court ruling striking down segregated seating on buses operating in Columbia, South Carolina, further stating that segregated seating in public transportation is illegal.[128]

White community leaders, elected officials and representatives from the Cities Transit bus company downplayed any concerns they may have had regarding the impact of the fledgling boycott. African American leaders reacted in the opposite manner, and on Tuesday the twenty-ninth, the Ministerial Alliance, a grouping of Black ministers, took up the subject at a regularly scheduled meeting held at the Bethel AME Church. At the urging of ministers C.K. Steele and James Hudson, the meeting was well attended.[129]

It was here, at Reverend Steele's church, that African Americans felt free to voice their anger over the slights and humiliations they received daily. Policies enacted by Cities Transit bus service came up for extended discussion considering the newly started boycott.

The Cities Transit bus company operated like bus service providers in other communities. The city or county did not directly operate the line, but rather Cities Transit carried out business under a franchise agreement. Today, we might use the term *lease operator* to describe the company. While Cities Transit was an independent operator, it was required to follow city ordinances and the terms of its contract. At the time, Tallahassee City Ordinance 741 (section 4) required Cities Transit to "make and enforce reasonable rules and regulations providing for the segregation of the human races when more than one race is transported on the same bus."[130]

Scholar Glenda Alice Rabby summarized the dilemma that the bus company found itself in. Black and White citizens were not able to sit next to each other. Painted in each bus was a white line. White riders sat in front of this line, Black riders behind the line. On predominantly Black routes, especially those running through the Florida A&M campus, this was especially upsetting to Black riders, who were often forced to stand when there were seats available. Black riders were also required to give up their seat should a White rider board a full bus.[131]

The result of the meeting on the morning of the twenty-ninth was the appointment of a nine-man group to meet with Tallahassee city manager Arvah Hopkins and bus company representative Charles Carter to discuss the recent events and air the grievances of the African American community. Both men appeared to pass the buck in the eyes of the Black delegation. Carter placed blame on the agreement with the city, while Hopkins stated he could not act without conferring with the city commission. Both statements were probably correct; however, in making them, the men showed an incredible lack of leadership and understanding of the situation. Receiving no satisfaction, the Black leaders left with little to report on at the larger meeting that evening.

That evening, a meeting was held at Bethel AME Church, where Reverend Steele provided locals with an update on what had happened and recent responses from city officials. Estimated attendance ranged from 450 to 500 persons. As Steele and the other leaders no doubt anticipated, the response was heated, so much so that when it came time to discuss the boycott of Cities Transit, the outcome was not in doubt. Local Black residents backed the student boycott and, in fact, enlarged the boycott to include all of Tallahassee, not just the college campus.[132]

Those in attendance knew something special was germinating. What they needed, however, was official leadership. The White establishment was firmly entrenched and did not appear willing to hold an open dialogue. It was important that Black citizens have an organization representing their side of the story. Reverend Steele and Robert Saunders, the Florida executive secretary of the NAACP, recommended the NAACP lead the Tallahassee bus boycott. Many residents balked at this idea, the primary reason being that the NAACP's aggressive reputation would allow White leaders to continue claiming that outside agitators were upsetting the racial harmony White leaders perceived to exist in Tallahassee. A local organization would be better able to negotiate and talk with city officials and residents.[133]

At the suggestion of Florida A&M University professor M.S. Thomas, the Inter-Civic Council (ICC) was born. Reverend Steele was elected ICC president. Despite his ties with the NAACP, he made sure it was known

Reverend Charles Kenzie Steele is shown outside the Bethel Missionary Baptist Church. Here, Steele organized a public meeting that led to Tallahassee African Americans backing the bus boycott organized by Florida A&M students. *Image Courtesy State Archives of Florida.*

this was not a new name for an old organization. As Steele later stated, the new organization "would include representatives from all of the civic organizations in town interested in racial progress."[134] In a 1976 interview, Reverend Steel told historian Gregory B. Padgett that the stated objectives of the ICC were:

> *To plan and execute civic, religious, scientific, educational and recreational programs for the benefit, enjoyment, general improvement and welfare of its members; to stimulate the attainment of high ideals and intellectual growth, to occupy a progressive and constructive place in the community; to develop friendship, peace and goodwill among men; and to advance the idea of the eternal fatherhood of God and the universal brotherhood of men.*[135]

This is not to say that the Tallahassee bus boycott and the ICC were not supported from outside the area. Cash donations were received from both the Montgomery Improvement Association and the NAACP. Martin Luther King Jr. made an appearance in the city, though this visit was not publicized. Again, locals did not want the White city leadership to proclaim this was a group of outside agitators causing problems. Years later, Reverend K.S. Dupont stated, "Montgomery was not a spark plug for Tallahassee. Tallahassee was its own spark plug."[136]

During the ICC's formative meeting a set of requests was drafted to end the bus boycott. As Gregory B. Padgett astutely points out, the ICC's "methods were nonviolent but directly confrontational."[137] The ICC proposed a three-point plan for city and bus company leaders to enact, the first point being that seating on city buses would be first come, first served; second, Black riders should be treated with courtesy by White drivers; and lastly, the bus company would agree to hire Black drivers to handle routes with primarily Black riders.[138]

Tallahassee and Cities Transit leaders continued to play hardball regarding the demands of the Black community, believing that Blacks were happy and would return to riding buses again shortly. By the end of May, no formal city reply had been crafted, and the sides were still at loggerheads. City and bus officials claimed not to know what was meant by seating on a first come, first served basis. Cities Transit spokespeople continued to hark back to their contractual terms rather than work with the two parties to find a solution.[139]

Perhaps in an attempt to lessen Black anger, the charges against Wilhelmina Jakes and Carrie Patterson were dropped and the women referred to Florida A&M for any disciplinary action. Tallahassee chief of police Frank Stoutamire publicly claimed this was a normal action when students were involved. From the beginning, law enforcement had been careful not to charge the students with violating any segregation ordinance. By not filing formal charges, police left little grounds for legal action on the students' behalf in challenging local laws.[140]

Another way White leadership attempted to deal with the emerging boycott was to go around the appointed leaders and attempt to negotiate with those whom they had dealt with in the past. On Saturday, June 2, city leaders met with fifteen Black citizens at Capital City Bank to try to work out an agreement to end the boycott. Only one of the fifteen African Americans in attendance was an ICC member: David Brooks.

Reverend Steele was out of town that day and publicly claimed he was not aware of the meeting. However, on Sunday, June 3, he preached a sermon about Judas Iscariot and betrayal. Those attending the service who also attended the secret meeting felt betrayed by Brooks and attacked by Steele.

Frank Stoutamire was a longtime law enforcement officer in Leon County. He served as sheriff from 1923 to 1953 and Tallahassee chief of police from 1953 to 1968. Stoutamire worked against protestors and those seeking to desegregate Tallahassee, often directing officers to arrest those seen as violating segregation ordinances. *Image courtesy State Archives of Florida.*

Steele continued to proclaim Brooks's and his own innocence in the subject of the sermon though the coincidence is hard to ignore.[141] Steele may have tipped his hand regarding his true feelings on this event when speaking to an NAACP gathering in Tampa, during which he discussed Uncle Toms. Steele stated,

> *The old Uncle Toms stooped, bowed, and conducted themselves to the end of obtaining some favors for the race. He felt that his conduct was necessary in an age of fear for the people of color in America, but this new Uncle Tom stoops, grins, and TALKS out of both sides of his mouth to feather his own nest, and to sell his own people down the river. I really don't know which group has been the most alarmed by our movement in Tallahassee, the white city officials, or the new Uncle Tom. They have both learned the hard way that Negro Tallahassee is not what she used to be.[142]*

That same Sunday, the *Tallahassee Democrat* published the city's response to the boycott demands. The city claimed that a policy of courtesy to all riders was already in place. The issue of Black bus drivers was a matter for Cities Transit and not for local government to involve itself in. Regarding the demand for "first come, first served" seating, the city put forth a half-hearted attempt at reconciliation, stating, "No member of either race must give up his seat on a crowded bus to another race." The city refused, however, to accept the idea of people of differing races sharing a multi-person seat. In its patronizing manner, the city claimed to "hope that the controversy will be promptly terminated so that [bus] service may continue and that the tension may be eased and there be restored the harmonious and cooperative spirit between White and Negro citizens which has made this a progressive, happy community."[143]

Again, elected officials underestimated the anger and resolve in the African American community. That evening, in a meeting attended by an estimated one thousand people, Reverend Steele ramped up tensions, stating that he would no longer accept segregation on buses and that he believed Black Tallahassee residents were willing to walk. Those in attendance backed Steele.

The following morning, the ICC presented a resolution to the city commission, again demanding the right to "sit wherever they choose on any bus or busses," courteous and equal service from bus drivers and the hiring of Black bus drivers. As the resolution stated, it was a request for commissioners to make the "morally right decision." Commissioners took ten minutes to deny the resolution. They went so far as to allow Cities Transit to discontinue service to the unprofitable Florida A&M and Frenchtown routes. The newspaper aligned itself with the commission, editorializing that Blacks "have been unreasonable and have used ill-advised procedures." Editor Malcolm Johnson agreed with the decision on bus routes, claiming, "Suspension or outright cancellation of the service will remove a source of strife and let things cool off."[144]

As the boycott continued through June, revenues and profits for the bus company and city continued to decline. One estimate put the revenue decline at more than 60 percent. On June 12, the city commission granted Cities Transit a five-cent fare increase and lowered the company's franchise fee from 3 percent to only .5 percent.[145]

The bus boycott was pitting three distinct interests against each other and was showing the power of an entrenched group not wanting to change. The city commission was attempting to keep racial segregation as the norm; African Americans were attempting to flex their political and economic muscles to end a written policy of segregation, with the full understanding

Seth Gaines was an independent taxi driver in Tallahassee during the 1940s and 1950s. Gaines was hired by Cities Transit as a bus driver in response to the local bus boycott. *Photo courtesy State Archives of Florida.*

that racism would not thereby vanish; and Cities Transit, in their defense, was caught in the middle. Until the city commission amended the company's contract, it legally could not allow integrated seating, even if it wished to. Cities Transit did have the ability to enact the other two requests, if it had chosen to. It is not clear, however, that management wished to do so.

As the boycott continued throughout the summer months, Cities Transit received approval to shut down all service in Tallahassee if ridership did not increase. It was estimated that 60 to 70 percent of riders were Black and that more than 90 percent of Black riders were supporting the boycott. At midnight on June 30, Cities Transit shut down bus operations. In response to the stoppage of service, the city commission, again with a lack of understanding or concern, issued a statement saying that local Blacks were being misled by a group, "many of whom are newcomers to Tallahassee, and who apparently have no feeling of responsibility to the community, the general public or even members of their own race." ICC leaders assured boycott supporters that they would have transportation to work, to shop and for other needs.[146]

Throughout the early days of the boycott, African Americans continued to arrive at their jobs, despite the obstacle thrown in their way. Understanding

Left to right: Reverend Joseph Metz Rollins, Florida A&M professor of education Edwin F. Norwood Sr. and Reverend C.K. Steele were three of the leading civil rights activists in Tallahassee. Norwood served time as president of the local branch of the NAACP. *Image courtesy State Archives of Florida.*

the difficult situation the boycott caused for many locals, members of the ICC formed a transportation committee, with Dan Speed elected as chair. Speed and his committee were able to recruit sixty-five volunteer drivers to operate a carpool, filling the demand for transportation created when the boycott began. Tallahassee had strict rules regarding carpooling, taxis and cars for hire. Riders were instructed not to provide any payment to drivers. Instead, if riders wished, they could donate to the ICC, which would be able to assist drivers with expenses.[147]

As they should have expected, ICC drivers and their passengers were the target of police harassment. Drivers were pulled over for minor or imaginary offenses. Traffic citations and arrests were common. Drivers were often taken to police headquarters for questioning in an attempt to break the carpool. Reverend Steele himself was arrested three times in a single day.[148]

These harassment efforts were a help, but the city wanted something with a real bite to put an end to the ICC-led carpool. City attorney James Messer was asked to investigate the issue and develop a plan. Messer determined that the carpool might violate state law governing cars for hire. Because the carpool drivers did not satisfy the state-mandated requirements for operating a "for hire car"—holding a special type of license, registration, insurance and displaying a required car tag—they were in violation of the state tag law. Messer requested state attorney general Richard Ervin's legal opinion.[149]

Tallahassee police did not refrain from stopping, detaining and arresting drivers suspected of participating in the carpool effort. Police chief Stoutamire denied any coordinated attempt at intimidation, a claim that nobody could have believed. To help with planned legal defenses, the ICC announced a $20,000 legal defense fund.[150]

In what might have been considered a public relations attempt, the chamber of commerce, along with Cities Transit management, announced that beginning on August 2, bus services would be provided. Smaller buses and revised routes were announced. Bus routes on the Florida A&M campus and the Frenchtown route would only be operated if there was demand. Cities Transit did hire several African American drivers for select routes; however, segregation was still enforced. The city and the bus company were still unresponsive.[151]

As the legal battle went on, state charges for tag law violations against carpool drivers were dropped, only to be replaced with a local ordinance violation for operating an illegal transportation system. Observers were not fooled by this move. By circumventing state courts, the city hoped to reduce the possibility of appeal. After hearing pretrial testimony, Judge John Rudd claimed he would not hear any arguments on the topics of segregation or integration. The trial would be about only the legality of the carpool. In total, twenty-two persons were to stand trial.[152]

The trial began on October 17, with the city charging the ICC with operating an illegal commercial transportation business that competed successfully with the exclusive contract of Cities Transit. The city argued that in three months, the ICC had received over $8,000 in revenue. The city produced more than seventy-five witnesses, many of whom admitted to donating funds to the carpool program at various ICC events. No law enforcement witnesses were able to state that they saw money changing hands between riders and drivers.[153]

The trial concluded on October 21, and Judge Rudd took less than fifteen minutes to announce his verdict. All defendants were found guilty. The sentence for each, including Reverend Steele, was a suspended sixty-day jail sentence and a $1,000 fine. The $22,000 cumulative fine seemed to be an effort to bankrupt the ICC and bring an end to the boycott on terms favorable to the city and the White-owned Cities Transit.[154]

As throughout the entire boycott, White officials underestimated the support of Black residents for the cause. Elected officials believed that breaking the carpool would force Black riders back on buses. While Black ridership did marginally increase, what White elected officials and bus representatives failed to consider was that almost all those riders only rode Black-driven routes. Florida A&M students continued a near-full boycott.[155]

The *Tallahassee Democrat* continued to blow the horn of the "golden age of racial harmony," claiming, "It's just a fight between the bus company and the Negroes. If it weren't for these out-of-towners sticking their noses into it, it would have been all over with. There is no tension here, we have always gotten along." Henry Gitano, in the *Militant*, replied that the lack of tension "was actually the silent suffering of insults and degradation for decades."[156]

Segregationists across the country were dealt a blow on November 13, 1956, when the United States Supreme Court upheld a lower court ruling in the case of *Browder v. Gayle* stating that segregationist bus laws in Alabama were unconstitutional. This ruling would not end segregated busing, but it certainly put the writing on the wall for cities like Tallahassee.[157]

Despite victory in Alabama, the ICC was facing a considerable problem in Tallahassee. Nobody was certain what the ruling meant in other states. Tallahassee mayor John Y. Humphress went so far as to ask locals and the bus company to cooperate in maintaining the status quo, segregation.[158]

With the United States Supreme Court decision in *Browder*, the ICC was faced with segregation ordinances still on the books but a local populace, now without the convenience of the carpool system, wanting to ride the buses. On December 20, ICC members voted to end the boycott. African Americans would immediately return to riding Cities Transit buses, but in a nonsegregated manner.

Following a lead from Blacks in Montgomery, Alabama, the ICC directed riders to sit closer to the front and withhold retaliation against violence toward them and promised legal support should police arrest any riders. Local Black religious leaders and those from the ICC also participated in riding buses. Always fast to support segregation, the *Tallahassee Democrat* reported on December 24, 1956, that "Negro domestics were riding at the rear of the bus," a claim that seems highly unlikely in light of the recent struggles.[159]

Tallahassee elected officials were not ready to concede defeat. Having already battled the ICC and Black locals, the city commission turned its anger on Cities Transit. Commissioners sent a formal order to Cities Transit

Local civil rights leaders played a participating role in the bus boycotts. Reverend C.K. Steele, Reverend H. McNeal Harris and Reverend A.C. Redd sat in front of the segregation line, as shown in this December 1956 photo. Local authorities often turned their frustration on not just African Americans but also Cities Transit employees for failing to enforce segregation laws. *Image courtesy State Archives of Florida.*

management requiring them and their drivers to enforce the local segregation ordinance or risk forfeiting their franchise. The bus company was clearly caught in a difficult situation and, in many ways, was being scapegoated by both the city and ICC.

Cities Transit stated it would seek court guidance as to whether the *Browder* ruling applied to Florida law and the Tallahassee ordinance specifically. On December 26, the city commission further antagonized both the bus company and African American riders by suspending the Cities Transit franchise in the "best interest of peace and harmony." Cities Transit fired back, stating the suspension did not follow contractual requirements and was thus illegal.[160]

Ratcheting up the tensions further, on December 27, police chief Stoutamire had officers arrest Cities Transit manager Charles Carter and nine drivers for failure to enforce the segregation ordinance. Each was

A late December demonstration that would have seen African American bus riders seated near the front of buses was abruptly called off when more than two hundred White counterprotestors, including many young men who were openly discussing their plans, gathered near the Park Avenue and Monroe Street bus stop. *Image courtesy State Archives of Florida.*

released on payment of a one-hundred-dollar bond. That evening, Judge Dozier Devane ruled against Tallahassee in a temporary injunction, stopping the city's interference in bus operations until a further decision came from the courts.[161]

White violence became a more common occurrence after Christmas, with mobs of mostly young White men threatening Blacks wishing to ride buses. In response to the situation, on December 31, Governor Leroy Collins used his authority to suspend bus service in Tallahassee, claiming that the segregation issue had created a "climate of racial tension between the White and Negro citizens." The possibility of violence, he continued, "seriously threatens the lives and well-being of citizens of both races as well as the peace, tranquility, and good order of the community." Violence continued into the new year. On January 2, 1957, a cross was burned on the lawn of C.K. Steele, Black businesses were targeted with vandalism and Black-owned cars had windows smashed out.[162]

Tensions remained high into the second week of January, when the Tallahassee city commission again failed to exhibit sound leadership. On January 7, commissioners declared a repeal of segregated bus seating. Instead, they formulated what became known as a seat assignment plan, which would take effect when Governor Collins lifted his suspension. Under this plan, bus drivers would assign seating for "maximum health and safety" of riders. Those who refused their assigned seat faced a maximum fine of $500 and/or sixty days in jail. Black riders and the ICC certainly saw through this plan. This would lead to non-ordinance segregation.[163]

On January 12, Governor Collins lifted his bus suspension, allowing the new seat assignment plan to go into effect. One week, later six students—three Florida A&M students and three from Florida State University—boarded a bus, and as might have been expected, the White students were given front seats and the Black students assigned seats in the rear of the bus. During the ride, three students exchanged sets, purposefully creating seats filled by both Black and White riders. When they refused the driver's order to return to their assigned seats, they were arrested and charged with violating the new ordinance.[164]

When the cases of Joe Spagna and John Herndon from Florida State University, and Florida A&M student Leonard Speed (the son of ICC official Reverend Dan Speed) came to trial, the defendants were quickly found guilty by Judge John Rudd. All received the maximum penalty of $500 and sixty days in jail. Rudd admonished the students, saying they should not attempt to be "modern fly-by-night martyrs." All three were released on bail pending appeal. Appeals to both the Florida Supreme Court and the United States Supreme Court were denied. Warrants were issued for the three young men. Speed and Herndon surrendered, but Joe Spagna jumped bail, leaving the state and not serving his sentence.[165]

Francisco Rodriguez, the attorney for both Speed and Herndon, appealed to the city commission for clemency on the jail terms. At a special hearing on April 10, Judge Rudd appeared and recommended suspending the sentences of the two youths, who had already served fifteen days. Rudd continued the theme of outside agitators in his comments, stating these two young men "were not the real culprits, but were the victims of circumstances and acted under the influence of persons and organizations who gave little or no consideration to the public interest or the interest of the defendants." Commissioners agreed, and the students were released.[166]

Several successes arose from the boycott. In less than one year's time, but at the cost of considerable effort, Black riders were allowed to sit on

Francisco Rodriguez (*left, with Reverend C.K. Steele and Reverend Daniel B. Speed*) often served as an attorney for those arrested while participating in civil rights protests in Leon County. He was also active in the legal efforts to desegregate schools in Florida in the post–*Brown v. Board of Education* era. *Image courtesy State Archives of Florida.*

the bus where they desired without legal resistance. Cities Transit was responsive and hired Black drivers for not just African American routes. Further, harassment and humiliation of Black riders lessened but was not eliminated. Black riders were treated with more courtesy and respect than they had been prior to the boycott. These successes led to further desegregation efforts throughout the city. The self-esteem of Black Tallahassee residents increased, and they came to fully understand they were equal to White residents. By working together, Black residents were able to effect lasting change. Though it took time, White residents began to understand and accept this as well.[167]

Today, this event does not receive a large amount of formal commemoration in Tallahassee, but there are several places of honor visitors should seek. At the corner of East Jefferson Street and South Monroe Street is the Tallahassee Civil Rights Heritage Walk. This sidewalk memorial was unveiled on September 30, 2013, and was created by the Florida State University Master Craftsman Studio. It consists of sixteen terrazzo tiles that commemorate more than fifty civil rights activists, including those of the 1956 bus boycott. In addition, the main terminal for Tallahassee city buses is

In honor of his courageous efforts, in 1985, the Tallahassee City Bus Terminal was named the C.K. Steele Plaza. Unveiled at the Plaza was a bronze statue of Reverend Steele, cast by artist David Lowe. Also located at the Steele Plaza is a plaque dedicated to Rosa Parks. *Image courtesy State Archives of Florida.*

named in honor of Reverend Charles Kenzie Steele. At this site is a bronze sculpture, created by artist David Lowe, in honor of the man who helped lead Tallahassee's Black citizens through the bus boycott, ensuring that they would not ride in humiliation.[168]

Chapter 4

"WE HAVE NEVER WORKED IN ONE AS LAWLESS AS THIS"

So stated Dr. Martin Luther King in the spring of 1964, describing the community of St. Augustine, Florida.[169]

Tensions across the country were at a breaking point as civil rights protestors marched against segregationists through many communities in the South. While the White leadership often bemoaned outside agitators, claiming their towns did not have racial strife, these claims were always false. St. Augustine, Florida, a community highly dependent on tourism, was one of these towns. And while it is true that outsiders such as the Reverends Fred Shuttleworth and Andrew Young, along with the likes of Hosea Williams and Dr. Martin Luther King Jr., provided an outside spark for local civil rights marchers, men such as Atlanta, Georgia–based Ku Klux Klan leader J.B. Stoner and segregationist leader Reverend Connie Lynch fanned the anger and hatred of local racists and segregationists. With the looming backdrop of the 1964 Civil Rights Act and the 1965 St. Augustine quadricentennial—celebrating the four-hundredth anniversary of Spanish settlement in the city—set to take place, the community was a powder keg ready to explode should a match be lit.

St. Augustine of the early 1960s was the usual southern mix, with a White community accustomed to feeling in control that saw "Blacks as inferior" and "paternalistically kept them in their place, economically and socially."[170] Much as White Tallahassee leaders in the 1950s professed the "golden age of racial harmony," St. Augustine was still the same way a decade later.

Dr. David R. Colburn describes the situation Black residents found themselves seemingly locked into:

> *Segregation denied blacks full and equal access to the railroad station, bus depot, restrooms, drinking fountains, public schools, city hospital, and library, and blacks attended separate churches. Blacks made a living in St. Augustine by waiting upon white needs as servants, maids, migrant workers, tenant farmers, and menial laborers, and the city's reliance on the tourist industry emphasized dramatically that subordinate role. Black residents lived in the southwest section of the city and in an area just west of the city limits. Whites commonly referred to the section in the city as "colored town," although several white families also resided in the rather well-maintained area.*[171]

Claudia Slate adds, "Content with their situation, whites remained unaware of the emerging racial discontent."[172]

One man in particular was not content with this situation: Dr. Robert Hayling. Hayling was the son of a faculty member at the Tallahassee-based Florida A&M University (FAMU). He received his undergraduate degree from FAMU and his dental degree from Nashville, Tennessee–based Meharry Medical College before returning to Florida and taking up residence in St. Augustine, where he took over an existing practice.[173]

It can be difficult to pinpoint just what, or who, the root causes of protest movements are. While Black residents in St. Augustine had been held down in a position of inferiority and servitude since the end of Reconstruction, there can be little doubt that the rapidly approaching quadricentennial celebration and the debates in Washington, D.C., over the proposed Civil Rights Act provided an opening for local African Americans to put their case on display, and not just for a state- or even country-wide audience: this time, the world would be watching.

The quadricentennial was planned to celebrate the four-hundredth anniversary of Spanish settlement of the city. The event that ultimately occurred in September 1965 has been described by historian Reiko Hillyer as

> *a ten-day fiesta whose schedule included a State of Florida Day, a Mexican Day, a performance by a Spanish dance troupe, strolling troubadours, fireworks, a Hispanic fashion show, and sword-fighting displays. Guests included delegations from Spain and Puerto Rico, such as a descendant of the Spanish explorer Pedro Menendez and a "typical Spanish family" from*

Left: California Ku Klux Klan member Connie Lynch, seen here leading a rally at the St. Augustine Public Market, served as an outside agitator for the local pro-segregation population. *Image courtesy State Archives of Florida.*

Opposite: Ralph Abernathy (*left*) and Martin Luther King Jr. were outside agitators for the desegregation movement in St. Augustine. Abernathy would follow in the steps of King, becoming the second president of the Southern Christian Leadership Conference after King's assassination in 1968. *Image courtesy State Archives of Florida.*

Menendez's hometown of Aviles. Interpreting the event as an opportunity to solidify the friendship between the United States and Spanish-speaking countries, Florida governor W. Haydon Burns toasted "those nations whose historic and cultural bonds are tied together and deep-rooted, as is the case between the people of Spain and the United States," and declared that inter-American goodwill was essential to the peace and prosperity of the post-World War II world.[174]

The National Association for the Advancement of Colored People (NAACP) and the Southern Christian Leadership Conference (SCLC) saw something different in the quadricentennial. Ralph Abernathy, who was a close associate of Dr. Martin Luther King Jr. and would become president of the SCLC after King's 1968 assassination, described what they saw and heard: "We were always on the lookout for localities that had particularly harsh regimes, cities that were oppressive beyond the ordinary limits of southern society....So we sought out St. Augustine—or to be more precise, St. Augustine sought out us."[175]

In 1964, residents of St. Augustine were crying out, albeit for different things. The business community was calling for federal backing and financial

support for the quadricentennial. The event could prove a massive jolt to an already strong tourist economy. African American residents were calling for a place at the economic table. They were seeking equal opportunity in education, jobs, beach access, shopping and dining. They wanted an opportunity to participate in the quadricentennial. The cries of African American residents were ignored by local White leaders.

Not only were the requests of African Americans ignored, but many city residents were also actively conservative and anti-segregation. Groups such as the John Birch Society, the Ku Klux Klan, the White Citizens' Council and the Florida Coalition of Patriotic Societies had footholds in the town. Members of these organizations led civic and business groups, ensuring their support.[176] To further the cause of White supremacy, the local sheriff, L.O. Davis, was a staunch opponent of civil rights and desegregation. "Davis saw the civil rights movement as a Communist conspiracy to take over the United States and he had no doubt that Martin Luther King was a communist."[177] Davis was closely allied to known anti–civil rights activist Holstead "Hoss" Manucy. Manucy, who had a violent temper, was the known leader of the Ancient City Gun Club, a group widely considered a front for Klan membership and activities.[178]

Dr. Robert Hayling (*left*) is shown with SCLC member Len Murray during the "long hot summer" of 1964. Hayling, a local dentist, served as the spark that helped ignite in local African Americans the desire to call for— and fight for, when necessary—their civil rights. *Image courtesy State Archives of Florida.*

With these obstacles in front of them, local African Americans found themselves in a difficult situation, even as various civil rights measures were passed by the United States Congress. All was not lost for them, however, as the newly arrived dentist, Dr. Robert Hayling, was determined to do something. Hayling joined the local branch of the NAACP, a group of no more than thirty members.

Leadership in the local NAACP branch at the time was rather timid. Branch leaders Fannie Fullerwood and Elizabeth Hawthorne were not of the confrontational mind. Rather, they attempted to work with local White leaders and the White business community. Because of this nonconfrontational attitude, the Black community of St. Augustine gave the group little attention. If the group was not pushing for the "advancement" of Blacks, why should it be given support? This was the attitude Hayling set out to change.[179]

Hayling knew he had to attract the support of local youths, and in order to do so, he became an advisor to the local youth council of the NAACP. As he found with the broader NAACP, the youth council was quite small, comprised of fifteen members, the majority of whom were high school age, with only a small number of them attending Florida Memorial College.

Young Black residents of St. Augustine took to Robert Hayling. In him, they perhaps saw their own ideals. Hayling wished for an end to segregation and was a leader who understood that the passive tactics of Fullerwood and Hawthorne would not accomplish his goals. Hayling and his supporters knew they had a long and difficult road ahead of them. Not only did they have White opponents, but many in the Black community also expressed concerns about Hayling and his tactics. Many older residents considered him "new" and thought he didn't understand how St. Augustine worked. What these older residents did not understand was how Hayling, and a new generation of civil rights leaders and protestors, worked.[180]

The rapidly approaching 1965 quadricentennial was highly anticipated, not just on a local level but in Tallahassee and Washington, D.C., as well. Preparations for the celebration began at the federal level in 1962 with the establishment of the Quadricentennial Commission to help plan and oversee the event as a whole. The commission was to be comprised of four members of Congress, a representative from the Department of the Interior (which oversees the National Park Service and thus the Castillo de San Marcos in St. Augustine) and six appointees to be chosen by the president. Appealing for the creation of the commission, Congressman Billie Matthews put forth, "We, in Florida, believe that Saint Augustine, because of its more ancient history and identification with early colonial America, offers an equal if not better opportunity than Williamsburg [Virginia] to become a shrine for the preservation of values which have been most meaningful in our country's history."[181] To read this quote understanding the events that transpired over the next three years surely calls into question which values Congressman Matthews meant.

At Dr. Hayling's urging, the local NAACP began addressing the continued situation with officials in Washington, D.C. In March 1963, Fullerwood and Hawthorne sent a letter to the attention of Vice President Lyndon Johnson, alerting him of the repressive conditions in St. Augustine and urging him to cancel his planned visit to the city. In part, the letter read, "Please, allow us to inform you that the planning committee and the welcoming committee for this event do not include representation from all the population segments of the city. In short, they are segregated."[182] Fullerwood and Hawthorne complained of several issues, including continued segregation, city leaders' refusal to establish any kind of biracial commission and the city's recent failure to issue a parade permit to Black leaders in order for them to protest segregation. Vice President Johnson replied that he would not take part in a segregated event. With Johnson's words in mind, city leaders rapidly put together a committee, including twelve local African Americans not associated with the NAACP. At the request of national NAACP president Roy Wilkins, Hayling accepted this outcome. The results were predictable.[183]

Vice President Johnson arrived in St. Augustine in March 1963 to help dedicate a Spanish landmark. During a dinner with Johnson, Black attendees were seated together, separated from the vice president, who did not speak with them. To add further insult, Johnson's press secretary, George Reedy, was to meet with local Black leaders along with members of the city commission the following day. When the Black representatives arrived at the appointed hour, they were met by St. Augustine city manager Charles Barrier, his secretary and a tape recorder—no members of the Johnson team, no Washington, D.C. press and no members of the city commission, as promised. Rather, Barrier stated he would take a transcript of the recording of the meeting back to the city commission. Faced with no other options, the Black leaders discussed the lack of opportunities for Blacks to work in city government, continued segregation in public and private facilities and a lack of affordable housing.[184]

Little changed as the visit from Vice President Johnson became a memory. In early May, again at the urging of Dr. Hayling, local NAACP leaders Fullerwood and Hawthorne took to writing to Washington, D.C. This time, they reached out to President John F. Kennedy, requesting that he come out in opposition of a $350,000 federal grant to help support the quadricentennial. They wrote that the United States could "prove to the Communists and the entire world that America's oldest city can truly be a showcase of democracy."[185] Fullerwood and Hawthorne cited local concerns such as continued segregation, lack of city job opportunities and the failure of elected officials to meet with Black leaders after the vice president's visit. The Kennedy administration did not respond.

While the president did not reply, city leaders forcefully did. When it came to employment, they stated that Black residents could apply for any job opening and that 27 of 150 city jobs were held by Blacks. The city failed to point out that almost all 27 of these workers were garbage men or low-level secretaries. The city also stated that because schools were operated by the St. Johns County School Board, this issue was beyond its control. It further made the claim that privately owned businesses were within their rights to serve who they wished. The city, in its final claim, asserted that the city commission had not refused to meet with Black leaders and that commissioners had not promised to attend the meeting after the vice president's visit. Not only were local politicians upset, but so were many local business owners. About the NAACP asking for Kennedy to intervene, Ralph Abernathy has written, "When this attempt at intervention became public knowledge, the white businessmen of St. Augustine were furious. The establishment had been wounded in the most vital part of its anatomy—its pocketbook."[186]

As the Florida weather grew warmer, tensions rose on both sides. Mayor Joseph Shelley dug in, believing the entire civil rights movement was backed by Communists. However, Shelley, a medical doctor, proved an interesting case. Most of his patients were Black and it appears they received proper care. He believed that Blacks needed better jobs and more education. In return, he received Black support during the 1963 elections. What Shelley did not, and could not, believe was that the races were equal. He has been quoted as saying, "I consider myself a segregationist. God segregated the races, as far as I'm concerned when he made skins a different color. You don't find bluebirds and redbirds feeding together at the same trough, and you certainly don't see them breeding together."[187]

Hayling and his young followers took to the streets beginning on June 25, 1963. In a scene that would become familiar throughout the country, Black teenagers paraded in front of F.W. Woolworth carrying signs reading, "If we spend money here why can't we eat here?" Members of the NAACP Youth Council picketed at the St. Augustine Civic Center. The following day, more than twenty teenagers participated in sit-ins at Service Drugs, McCrory's and Woolworths, causing all three locations to close their lunch counters.[188]

Woolworths stores and lunch counters across the South served as a focal point in civil rights protests. St. Augustine was no different. This F.W. Woolworth was located across King Street from the Plaza and Public Market. *Image courtesy State Archives of Florida.*

Sit-ins continued, and the response became hardened. In July, a sit-in resulted in the arrest of sixteen, including seven juveniles. County judge Charles Mathis, a civil rights opponent who, like Mayor Shelley, believed integration to be a Communist plot, cracked down on the juveniles and their families. He stated he would release the children into parental custody only if the parents stated they would keep them away from any future demonstrations. While three families agreed to the terms, four did not, and the teens remained in jail.

In response to Mathis's ruling, more than one hundred protestors marched at the county jail the following evening, leading to a clash with law enforcement. In what was no doubt a gross exaggeration, Sheriff L.O. Davis claimed the demonstration was "worse than anything I've seen since Birmingham." Law enforcement attacked protestors with nightsticks. The press was not immune from segregationist rage either as a photographer had his camera forcibly seized.[189]

Judge Mathis was not interested in conflict resolution and threw additional gasoline on the smoldering fire. In response to the demonstration and in cooperation with Sheriff Davis, Mathis transferred the teens to state incarceration. Audrey Nell Edwards and Jo Ann Anderson were sent to Ocala Correctional School for Girls, while Samuel White and Willie Carl Singleton were taken to the Florida Industrial School for Boys. Officials at both facilities balked at taking in these teens for misdemeanors, and Florida attorney general James Kynes asked the judge to reconsider this action. Even the pressure from Florida Gator standout and former professional football player Kynes could not change Judge Mathis's mind. The youths would only be freed months later after their cause became national news and Governor Ferris Bryant convened the Correctional Institutions Board before signing a release.[190]

Race relations continued to decline. The St. Johns Chapter of the Florida Coalition of Patriotic Societies, the local chapter of the John Birch Society, was formed in 1963. While only having approximately fifty active members, the society's reach and influence was felt throughout the community. The society was led by Dr. Hardgrove Norris. With conservative leadership—Norris, Sheriff Davis, Mayor Shelley and men such as Hoss Manucy—aligned against Robert Hayling, dozens of local youths and the NAACP, the city was truly at a dangerous point. As Ron Jackson, a prominent St. Augustine veterinarian, phrased it: "You got pushed to one side or the other. If you tried to stay in the middle your friends became your enemies."[191]

Right: University of Florida Athletic Hall of Fame member James Kynes served as Florida governor Farris Bryant's executive assistant before being appointed attorney general in 1964. He lost his bid to be elected for a full term and left office in 1965. *Image courtesy State Archives of Florida.*

Below: Shed Dawson (*left*) and John L. White (*right*), shown here with NBC News correspondent Tom Streithorst, were typical of the young protestors who ran afoul of local segregationists in St. Augustine. *Image courtesy State Archives of Florida.*

Labor Day 1963 raised the bar for tensions within the city. More than 125 NAACP members and supporters converged on the Plaza de la Constitución to protest continued discrimination and the city council's unwillingness to appoint a biracial commission. Armed police were quickly summoned to break up the protest. Wielding cattle prods, they quickly began beating marchers, including Reverend Goldie Eubanks, who was subsequently arrested and found guilty of resisting arrest. He would be sentenced to six months' jail time.[192]

Police violence toward protestors continued to increase as fall arrived. Police chief Virgil Stuart and Sheriff L.O. Davis seemed to turn a blind eye, believing that the protestors were communists and Blacks and Whites were not equals. When the NAACP applied for a parade permit to protest police violence on September 21, not only was the permit denied, but permits for "all parades, demonstrations, and large public gatherings were…suspended indefinitely."[193]

The time for peaceful discussion was rapidly passing, even though White leaders seemed not to take notice. Mayor Shelley had gone so far as to write to a supporter about the situation, "I think one of the best indications of the way the Negro and white citizen feel towards each other has been the fact that in spite of every effort by the leaders of the NAACP to stir up large demonstrations and incidents, they have failed miserably." Just as White leaders in Tallahassee had underestimated the resolve of African Americans in their community, White leaders in St. Augustine did not understand the needs of African Americans in their city. Not only were they misreading the Black residents, but they could not see the impact their local events were having around the country.[194]

The September 1963 arrival of Connie Lynch, "the modern Klan's most notorious evangelist" from California, driving his pink Cadillac, would push St. Augustine race relations to an even more violent stage. The "Reverend" Lynch was a known KKK leader with violent tendencies. Lynch met with Klan members in Jacksonville, convincing them to support fellow Klan members to the south. On the eighteenth, more than three hundred Klan members and observers met for a rally and cross burning north of the city limits. Here, Lynch was introduced to those in attendance. The crowd roared approval as he heaped praise on the bomber who killed four young girls in Birmingham.[195]

Lynch then verbally attacked Robert Hayling, calling him a "burr-headed bastard of a dentist." He continued, "If you were half the men you claim to be you'd kill him before sunup."[196] He left the stage having worked the white-robed onlookers into a frenzy.

Klansman Connie Lynch encouraged local segregationists and Klan members to kill Dr. Robert Hayling while speaking during a Klan rally and cross burning. *Image courtesy State Archives of Florida.*

In an act that may have been called bravery or stupidity, Hayling and several other Black men witnessed the events of the evening. When they were discovered, the four men were savagely beaten. Women in the crowd were yelling, "Castrate the bastards," "Kick their balls out" and "Knock their heads off!" The men were piled like wood on a fire while a Klan member was sent to acquire gasoline. One Klansman was heard to say, "Did you ever smell a _____ burn?…It's a mighty sweet smell."[197]

Another spy in attendance left quickly and alerted authorities, including Sheriff Davis, who arrived and, with his deputies, prevented a multiple murder. Hayling and his associates were taken to Flagler Hospital to receive care for their wounds while Davis made a halfhearted arrest of four men. Between the perpetrators being hooded and Hayling having been beaten so badly, Hayling and the other men were unable to identify their attackers. As might have been anticipated, the case against the Klansmen was dismissed. Hayling, however, was found guilty of assault by the all-

White jury. For his "crime" he received a one-hundred-dollar fine and no jail time.[198]

Violence continued, reaching another crescendo on October 25. That evening, Holstead D. Manucy, son of Holstead R. "Hoss" Manucy, the reputed Klan leader, and his friends William Kinard, Dixon Stanford (a.k.a Dixon Wilson) and James E. Scaff were driving through the Lincolnshire section of St. Augustine, a traditionally Black neighborhood. Kinard held a loaded shotgun in his hands, evidently looking for trouble. Without warning, ten shots were fired from within, or near, a house on Palm Street. One of the blasts hit and ultimately killed Kinard. When struck, Kinard convulsed and fired his shotgun, shooting a hole through the roof of the car. Manucy provided law enforcement with an obviously false story that the young men had been dove hunting when the incident took place. Several Black residents, including Reverend Goldie Eubanks, were arrested, though police had no physical evidence. No charges were filed.[199]

Funeral services for William Kinard were held at the local Evergreen Cemetery on October 28 with more than two hundred Klansmen, including Connie Lynch, in attendance. That evening, Klansmen were out for revenge. Guns were fired at Black-owned homes and businesses. Blacks took to arming themselves. The streets became a dangerous place to be after dark.

The *St. Augustine Record* attempted to pin Kinard's death on radicals of both races, singling out the refusal of juveniles to obey court orders, civil rights meetings and Klan rallies. Mayor Shelley, having ignored the growing situation for months, attempted to calm residents, stating, "Do not be coerced or provoked into retaliation or acts of violence which can only result in bringing grief to yourselves and families." So concerned was he that he asked for, and received, thirteen state highway patrol officers and gave law enforcement orders to stop White attempts at intimidation in Black neighborhoods. His efforts provided short-term relief. However, he and the city commission still refused to appoint a biracial commission to discuss the underlying issues.[200]

During late 1963, Robert Hayling, Goldie Eubanks and the NAACP were dealt several setbacks, including the United States District Court refusing to issue an order preventing the arrest of civil rights demonstrators. Ultimately, both Hayling and Eubanks would resign, or were forced, from the NAACP. Their influence continued to be strong, however, particularly with younger Blacks, who were frustrated with the old, and seemingly unproductive, ways of the NAACP. Hayling and Eubanks would not disappear from the movement, and despite the hopes of White leaders, the movement was far from over. For many, it was just starting.[201]

Ralph Abernathy recalls those tense days,

> *At this point, the NAACP removed Dr. Hayling from his position with the local chapter, perhaps because local white leaders blamed him for the violence, and because the organization had in turn been judged guilty by association. Needless to say, we were shocked at this action. When Dr. Hayling and Goldie Eubanks resigned from the NAACP and asked to be affiliated with the SCLC, we accept them into our ranks, with the understanding that we would permit only nonviolent activities and nonviolent rhetoric.*[202]

During the first week of March 1964, the Florida branch of the Southern Christian Leadership Conference (SCLC) held its annual meeting in Orlando. Dr. Hayling, Reverend Eubanks, Henry Twine and several others, at the request of St. Augustine civil rights advocates, drove south to meet with Reverend C.T. Vivian, a member of the SCLC board of directors and a personal advisor to Martin Luther King Jr. At this meeting, they pled their case and argued for SCLC support in the face of dwindling NAACP backing. Reverend Vivian did not make any promises other than to visit the city at the conclusion of the conference.

Reverend Vivian held true to his word and visited the ancient city. Here, he found a deplorable situation. Conversations with local Black leaders and residents provided him with background on the city and what Black residents faced on a daily basis. The influence of outside White extremists coupled with the uncooperative city leadership made assistance inevitable. In his report to the SCLC board, he stated, "I recommended that the SCLC go into St. Augustine because of the desperate needs of local blacks and because we had not been in Florida before."[203]

St. Augustine was not new to the SCLC and had been watched by their board over the prior year. When it came time to vote, Dr. King and the SCLC board approved Reverend Vivian's proposal to go into St. Augustine. SCLC leaders wanted to provide "new dignity to the movement" and, with St. Augustine "pull the nonviolent thrust of the Negro back on center."[204]

SCLC leaders wasted no time in preparations and hit the ground running. Ralph Abernathy was to later write,

> *The first thing we did was send Willie Bolden, Robert Johnson, J.T. Johnson, Richard Gay, R.B. Cottonreader, Rev. C.T. Vivian, Rev. Fred Taylor, Rev. T.Y. Rogers, and other staff members to St. Augustine to "work-shop" all of the activists there so that they would know and*

*understand both the theory and the practice of nonviolent protest.…
Henceforth, everyone involved in SCLC-sponsored activities would go
unarmed and would submit to whatever indignity and physical abuse the
St. Augustine community could devise.*[205]

King and SCLC leaders saw several advantages to joining the efforts in St. Augustine, the first being that initial groundwork had already been laid by Dr. Hayling and the NAACP. Enthusiasm was already high. A second advantage was that White leadership continued to be in no mood for discussion, let alone compromise. The third advantage was the fragile tourist-based economy that the city depended on. The Florida East Coast Railway was a strong employer, but at that time, management and unions were in a bitter, and at times violent, stalemate over wages. Bad press from the FEC strike along with civil rights demonstrations could cripple the tourism industry, forcing the hand of officials. The final reason for SCLC enthusiasm about St. Augustine was the quadricentennial itself. The national publicity for the event "was particularly crucial to SCLC's effort to win support for the impending civil rights bill."[206]

Andrew Young, on seeing St. Augustine Black residents in action, and having taken part himself in a march that turned violent, agreed that the city could not be ignored. Its importance was crucial to passage of the civil rights bill then in Congress. As Young later wrote, "The demonstrations in St. Augustine might be necessary to overcome the filibuster that had been promised in the Senate. In addition, once in St. Augustine I realized we might as well see it through. It took remarkable courage for the people to decide to stand up for themselves after years of racial oppression. I couldn't say to them, 'Thanks, but no thanks, your sacrifice isn't politically necessary at this time.'" Reverend C.T. Vivian acknowledged the importance of St. Augustine in passing the bill, saying that "passage of the civil rights bill was a primary goal of the SCLC in St. Augustine."[207]

Despite the involvement of the SCLC, White community leadership continued to ignore requests for meetings. Sheriff Davis refused to provide protection for marchers, stating his men were powerless against a mob that might total five or six hundred. Davis's advice was not to march.[208]

While White residents and leaders continued to think that the protestors were being unreasonable, the SCLC believed otherwise. In contrast, the SCLC believed their demands to be quite modest and easily achievable with cooperation. "We asked for desegregation of public accommodations, the hiring of black policemen and firemen, and the establishment of a biracial commission to work out a plan for further desegregation of the city."[209]

Left: Andrew Young began his professional career as a pastor in Alabama. He would later serve as executive director of the SCLC, ambassador to the United Nations and mayor of Atlanta. *Image courtesy Library of Congress; Thomas J. O'Halloran, photographer.*

Right: Verle A. Pope, nicknamed the Lion of St. Johns, was a Florida state senator for twenty-four years. He was one of many who made the mistake of thinking race relations in St. Augustine were good before the arrival of outside agitators. *Image courtesy State Archives of Florida.*

With no obvious progress being made, the stalemate stretched on into the spring and summer months. White leaders continued to be blinded into thinking that race relations in St. Augustine had been good until the arrival of outside agitators. Florida state senator Verle A. Pope beat a familiar drum, stating, "We find ourselves beset by outside forces…when we had thought our race relations were among the finest."[210] Senator Pope, while far off base in his overriding beliefs, was partly correct in his statement. St. Augustine was to become "beset by outside forces," who, working with locals and SCLC leadership, kept the community in the news in a way elected and business leaders did not want.

Easter 1964 was rapidly approaching, and the SCLC hoped to capitalize on that holiday week and spring break in many northern colleges. In a carefully drafted letter that was distributed by many New England–based chapters of the SCLC, Robert Hayling stated, "This call is issued because of the particularly intolerable conditions within the city of St. Augustine. It may well be that the oldest historic city in the United States is one in which the patterns of discrimination, hatred, and violence are most deeply entrenched."[211] Martin Luther King Jr. and other leaders contacted supportive faculty and religious leaders asking for help in recruiting volunteers.

While searching the country for volunteers, the SCLC did exhibit concern over the potential for violence toward marchers. Andrew Young recalls trying to keep Martin Luther King out of St. Augustine. "We tried to keep Martin from coming to St. Augustine during the early phases of the campaign.… My fear was that the vigilante Klan types in the area were setting a trap to kill Martin. There were just too many fanatics in that town. The arch-racist J.B. Stoner, who ran for president on a white supremacist platform, was there stirring up things."[212]

King and the SCLC still believed in the tactic of nonviolence. As King stated, "The summer campaign model needed a purifying prelude in the sense of having a movement where Negroes remained completely nonviolent."[213] While their goals were to maintain a nonviolent demeanor, they had no faith that Whites would behave the same. In sending out the recruitment letters, the New Haven and Boston chapters of the SCLC warned that despite no violence and arrests being planned, "students must be willing to accept it," and telling them to be prepared to post bail if need be.[214]

As could be expected, not all who received the recruitment materials were friends to the cause. Mayor Shelley was alerted to the recruitment campaign by a student who provided a copy of the letter. The mayor quickly fired back, claiming there was no segregation in the city's public facilities and that Blacks were given equal opportunity for public jobs. The mayor's claims were without merit, as any resident of St. Augustine would have known.

Shortly after Shelley's attempt to squash recruitment efforts, he received a call at his desk from a reporter with the *Boston Globe*. One can only imagine the look on Joseph Shelley's face after hanging up the phone. The reporter asked if he knew a Mrs. Malcolm Peabody. Shelley answered as expected, in the negative. The reporter allowed that she was the wife of an Episcopal bishop and the mother of then Massachusetts governor Endicott Peabody. Mrs. Peabody planned to visit St. Augustine and participate in the Easter demonstrations. It is not hard to imagine the silence coming from the St. Augustine end of the phone call.

The northern reporter probed further, asking what Shelley and local law enforcement would do were she to violate any segregation laws. Shelley took the bait, as could be expected: "If she comes down and breaks the law, we are going to arrest her."[215] Yet again, White leaders failed to use any discretion, not comprehending the consequences of their words and actions.

Mrs. Peabody truly did not understand White St. Augustine and the events occurring in the town. She and her group arrived at the Jacksonville airport on the evening of March 29. A member of her party recalled her proclaiming on arrival in Florida, "I do not believe they [St. Augustine Whites] will deny me the pleasure of lunch with my Negro friend." Her driver, Hosea Williams, politely tried to correct her positive attitude.[216]

The following day would prove to be a long one for Peabody and her friends. After a meeting at the Zion Baptist Church, Mrs. Peabody and three other women, including Esther Burgess, the wife of the first elected Black bishop in the history of mainstream American churches, visited the downtown area, near the Plaza de la Constitución. The Plaza was home to a Confederate monument, a monument to Confederate general William Wing Loring and a marketplace that often went by the moniker "Old Slave Market," despite the questionable authenticity of that name. Their first stop was McCartney's lunch counter, where Mrs. Burgess ordered a fruit cup while the other three ladies ordered pancakes.[217]

Mrs. Burgess, being light skinned, was served with the same courtesy as her white companions. It was only when Mrs. Peabody commented to the waitress that it was nice they served Blacks that an issue arose. The startled waitress quickly left, and the women knew they would soon see a manager—or worse, police. When the manager arrived, he asked Mrs. Burgess if she was indeed Black, to which she answered in the affirmative. The women were quickly told to leave the premises, which they did, apparently without incident.[218]

The party next attempted to dine at Monson's Motor Lodge, directly across from the beautiful Matanzas River. They were stopped by staff, most likely owner and manager James Brock, and told they could eat outdoors in an area near the kitchen but could not dine inside. Brock told the group of ladies, "You and I will never live to see the day when people will be forced to take others into their hearts," to which Mrs. Peabody is said to have responded, "Where is your heart?" Rather than continue, the group moved along, seeing there was no reason to continue the discussion.[219]

If nothing else can be said of Mayor Shelley, he was true to his word regarding Mrs. Peabody. Despite their failure at the Monson, the seventy-two-year-old Mrs. Peabody joined an integrated group and entered the restaurant at the Ponce de Leon Motor Lodge. A short time after the group took their seats at a table near the bar, Sheriff Davis arrived, with two police dogs in tow, and requested that they leave or face arrest for being undesirable guests. Mrs. Peabody sat there resolutely, demanding the sheriff read her the statute he threatened them with. Unable to recite the law, the sheriff went to his patrol car to find the appropriate statute. Returning, he read the long legalese and threatened to place the entire group under arrest. Ultimately, Peabody and others left the scene but were not finished with their actions.

On March 31, the Peabody group entered the dining area at the exclusive Ponce de Leon Hotel and, despite requests from Florida governor Farris Bryant to local law enforcement, were arrested and transported to the St. Johns County Jail. Mrs. Peabody would be charged three times, with trespassing, being an undesirable guest and conspiracy. Her bond for the three charges was set at $450. After two nights spent in an overcrowded cell, she posted bail in order to give a presentation at the local First Baptist Church.

The press these arrests garnered was as expected. More than fifty reporters lined up at the jail seeking news and interviews with the key players. United States senators contacted the FBI and the Justice Department demanding information and to be assured of the safety of Mrs. Peabody. The *New York Times* ran an incredible photo of Mrs. Peabody in custody, showing Sheriff Davis beside her, cattle prod in one hand and a cigar in his mouth. It was reported that the newly created celebrity refused to bail herself out of jail while her friends remained.[220]

Mrs. Peabody's take on the situation was quoted in the *New York Times*: "We get involved in this because we think it'll go faster if we do it together.… It puts the spotlight on a city, and gives them unwelcome publicity. It lets people know that they [the Negroes] want a change and can't get it by themselves and that they need help." When Peabody left St. Augustine, the *New York Times* crowed, "Protestors Fail in St. Augustine." Peabody and Mayor Shelley later traded versions of events on NBC's *Today* show, with Peabody discussing the hatred and violence of the Oldest City. Shelley, for his part, continued to spread disinformation, claiming there were no racial problems in St. Augustine and that people like Hayling and Peabody did "a disservice not only to St. Augustine but the nation as a whole."[221]

Despite the efforts of northerners such as Mrs. Peabody and Mrs. Burgess, little improved for local Blacks. For many, conditions declined. The threat of economic retaliation was always present. Two Black employees were fired from the local Ford dealership: one for visiting the home of the owner, the second under suspicion of helping Hayling and the protestors. Flagler Hospital fired Lucille Plummer, the local SCLC treasurer, after warning her about her civil rights activities. White doctors took to the practice of

Reverend Martin Luther King Jr. attacked segregationist ideas in St. Augustine, including the idea that privately owned businesses had the right to serve, or not serve, whom they wished. Actions coming out of St. Augustine seen nationally were a considerable help in passing civil rights legislation in 1964. *Image courtesy State Archives of Florida.*

raising prices for Black patients, and Florida Memorial College warned students they would be suspended for participation in marches and demonstrations. The Fairchild Corporation brought all Black employees to a meeting, threatening that they would be fired if they participated in demonstrations. Sheriff Davis was known to notify the employers of those arrested, ensuring that extra-legal punishment was doled out.[222]

As the "long, hot summer" marched along, and the memory of Mrs. Malcom Peabody began to fade from people's immediate thoughts, the larger-than-life persona of Dr. Martin Luther King Jr. made a personal appearance in St. Augustine in June 1964. Not by accident, this visit coincided with an ongoing filibuster of the civil rights bill in the Senate. King believed White business owners and elected officials in St. Augustine would help focus the nation's attention further on the issue of race and, in particular, the issue of whether private businesses had the right to choose whom they allowed entrance and served.[223]

The belief that business owners had the right to serve—or, more precisely, not serve—whom they wished was a central factor in St. Augustine's conservative ranks. If the civil rights bill were to pass, their ability to keep their businesses segregated would be over. Reverend King and his allies in the SCLC knew this too well, and on June 11, 1964, they planned a visit to Monson's Motor Lodge.

Monson's Motor Lodge was owned and operated by James Brock. Brock and the Monson were specifically targeted out of a community full of smaller hotels and motor courts. Brock held standing within the hotel industry, having served as president of the St. Augustine Hotel, Motel and Restaurant Owners Association—a highly prestigious role in a community with an economy dependent on tourism—and, at the state level, the Florida Hotel and Motel Association. It was also known that a large group of out-of-town reporters was staying at the Monson. This made it easy to receive publicity. Brock was also considered to be a racist. Sheriff Davis had made Brock a "special deputy," and the *New York Times* reported that

James Brock and the Monson Motor Lodge served as a lightning rod in civil rights activities in St. Augustine, drawing the attention of both desegregation efforts and, later, the efforts of segregationists. The Monson was demolished in 2003 to make way for a Hilton. *Image courtesy the author.*

he had been "seen on a downtown street carrying a shotgun, a billy stick, a pistol, and a flashlight."[224]

Having a keen understanding of the value of the press, the SCLC had alerted members of the press in town that King and others would be visiting the Monson for lunch on the eleventh. Brock had been alerted as well and was ready for the inevitable confrontation.

King and a group of seven others, including Ralph Abernathy, arrived at the Monson Motor Lodge at 12:22 p.m. to eat lunch. The *New York Times* called the restaurant at the Monson one of the finest in St. Augustine. King, Abernathy and other staff members were met by owner James Brock, who stood on the red welcome mat outside the restaurant in an agitated manner.[225]

Knowing that something was going to occur, the crowd of onlookers had grown, and the press was on hand, hoping to witness and report a major story. Brock announced they were on private property and then asked Dr. King his name. "Martin King," the preacher replied. It has been reported that the two men tried to speak privately, but with the push of onlookers, it proved impossible. King told Brock, "You're going to have to integrate," and he asked if Brock understood the "humiliation our people have gone through." Brock replied that he would integrate his business if King could produce a "federal court order or if a group of St. Augustine businessmen prevail upon me," claiming that serving King and the others "would be detrimental to my business."[226]

The mood was then broken by a large White man yelling over the crowd to Brock, asking if he was open for business. When Brock answered in the affirmative, the man shoved his way through, pushing Abernathy into Dr.

King and calling King a "Black bastard." Brock, apparently growing weary of the ordeal, said to King, "I ask you on behalf of myself, my wife, and our two children, to leave." Despite the appeal, King had no intention of leaving. He was there to make a point. Brock, knowing he had been checkmated but seizing what he thought to be an opportunity, turned to the cameras, exclaiming, "I would like to invite my many friends throughout the country to visit Monson's. We expect to remain segregated."[227]

Sheriff Davis and police chief Stuart arrived and asked Brock if they were needed. King, Abernathy and others were arrested. King was placed in a patrol car just inches from Davis's German shepherd police dog. Charges included breach of the peace, conspiracy and trespass with malicious intent. According to Ralph Abernathy, "The whole process took less than an hour and our arrest made the evening news. That night, when we marched back to the slave market, we did so with less violence than before, perhaps because our arrests had to some degree satisfied the bloodlust of the mob."[228]

Martin Luther King Jr., Ralph Abernathy and others were arrested while trying to eat at the segregated restaurant in the Monson Motor Lodge. King was placed in a police car with a trained police dog, clearly an attempt to intimidate him. *Image courtesy State Archives of Florida.*

Tensions were rising, and according to eyewitness Claudia S. Slate, they exploded on the following day, June 12. Slate is the daughter of John Herbers, a reporter who was covering the unfolding St. Augustine drama at the time. Slate and family friend Frances McDowell were in downtown St. Augustine near Woolworths, across King Street from the Plaza. Slate reports that a group of civil rights demonstrators marched, carrying their large signs written on poster board. She recalls a group of White men bursting from another drug store and rushing the demonstrators. The men threw the demonstrators to the ground, beating them bloody with their own signs. Slate specifically recalls a policeman standing nearby doing nothing to stop the violence, which she said only ended when "the demonstrators did not return blow for blow" and "the thugs who had perpetrated the violence gained no satisfaction from their actions."[229]

That same day, June 12, is explained in a slightly different way by historians Taylor Branch and Franklin Reider, who discuss the night march of that day. Nearly two hundred participated in a pro-integration rally in the Plaza before dispersing. After they left, a larger group of Whites rallied behind the boisterous leaders J.B. Stoner. Stoner fired up the Whites protesters, yelling, "Tonight we are going to find out if white people have any rights. The coons have been parading around…for a long time." He carried on with his anti-integration rhetoric: "We're not gonna be put in chains by no Civil Rights bill now or any other time! There's nothing in the Constitution that gives Congress the authority to tell us we've go to eat with _____!" The Whites, protected by a police escort not provided to the Black marchers, paraded through the Lincolnville area of St. Augustine.[230]

If James Brock believed he was done with controversy, he was mistaken. Despite his reputation as a segregationist and having been deputized by Sheriff Davis, the townspeople did not cut Brock any slack. He and his family had received death threats, his business had been threatened and in the wake of a recent demonstration, his mother-in-law had suffered a heart attack. James Brock was a man on edge, and the events about to unfold on June 18 sent him over the edge.[231]

It was Hosea Williams who apparently hatched the plan to integrate the swimming pool at a local motel, and the Monson became the obvious target. In a planning meeting with Williams, Ralph Abernathy asked how they could accomplish this, because if a group of Blacks was seen walking through St. Augustine in their bathing suits, law enforcement would be quickly notified.[232]

Abernathy recalls Williams outlining the plan: "It's easy. I've already got it worked out. A couple of our White friends will register at the Monson Motor

Lodge. Then, we'll go by their rooms, one or two at a time. We'll change into bathing suits there and then step out the door and walk to the pool. It's just a few steps. Before they know we're there, we'll be paddling around the pool."[233]

When the Black protestors reached the pool, there were several White patrons swimming and enjoying themselves. When the protestors jumped into the pool, the White swimmers left quickly. As Abernathy said, "We weren't sure whether they got out because they didn't want to share the pool with us or because they knew that the fireworks were about to begin."[234]

The problem with Abernathy's account of the day is that it does not explain everything that occurred or how reporters and photographers would have known what was going to happen. Other sources must be examined to gain a wider perspective on the day.

Around 12:40 p.m. on June 18, an integrated group arrived at the Monson Motor Lodge with the goal of eating in the restaurant. This group included several rabbis who had been invited to St. Augustine by Dr. King personally. Brock, as earlier in the week, told the group that his establishment was segregated and that they were not welcome on the property. The rabbis refused to leave and then knelt in prayer. Brock, himself a known Baptist, snapped, grabbing at the rabbis and their group and physically shoving them away from his business and off the property.[235]

Only moments later, several young Blacks jumped into the Monson pool, drawing the already irate Brock's attention from the trespassing rabbis. Brock immediately began yelling at two White registered guests, "You're not putting these people in my pool." The White swimmers replied, "These are our guests, we are registered here, and want these people to swim with us."[236]

Brock ran back inside the building, returning shortly after with two large containers filled with what he claimed was acid. When the swimmers did not respond to his threats, Brock poured the contents of the containers in the pool, no doubt alarming the protestors. Ralph Abernathy recalls, "For a minute or so we were uneasy, but the stain disappeared before it spread to where we were standing in deep water. The manager knew at the same time we did that our skins weren't going to burn off our bodies, so he cursed and ran back into the building. Five minutes later we heard the distant wail of a siren that grew louder and louder."[237]

Brock had poured muriatic acid into his pool. Muriatic acid is a cleaner that is diluted with water for use. It is also used to help balance pH levels in swimming pools. While poisonous, diluted in a large amount of water in a well-ventilated outdoor swimming pool, the small amount Brock poured was unlikely to have caused any harm to the bathers.

When the police arrived, the scene devolved into a frenzy for the press. Reporters and camera operators captured the event firsthand. At first unsure of how to handle the situation, officer James Hewitt demanded the swimmers exit the pool to be arrested. Abernathy recalls that the water in the pool was a comfortable temperature and the swimmers moved to the middle of the pool, out of reach of the officers.

Receiving no cooperation from the swimmers, Officer Henry Billitz took off his shoes, jumped into the pool fully clothed and began fighting with the White swimmers, whom he apparently believed were instigators. Billitz's image, and the "swim-in" story, were later displayed in newspapers across the country, as an Associated Press journalist captured the action from poolside. The swimmers began exiting the pool, and all were arrested, many by state officers ordered to St. Augustine by Governor Farris Bryant.[238]

Seated across Avenida Menendez, watching the event unfold, were Martin Luther King, Ralph Abernathy and several aides. King was heard to say, "We are going to put Monson out of business."[239]

Later that year, Brock would explain his actions to a group of northern university students: "I stand for the free enterprise system, the right to refuse service, and States rights. All out for Goldwater."[240]

While swim-ins and marches were continuing, White leadership was beginning to turn. On June 17, state senator Verle Pope along with White St. Augustine business owners announced their plan to follow future federal legislation. Plans were also in place to introduce a biracial committee. Mayor Shelley remained unconvinced and wanted the SCLC to leave St. Augustine for a period of thirty days. Shelley's demands fell in line with grand jury recommendations that called for a biracial committee after a thirty-day cooling-off period with the SCLC and other outside forces removing themselves from the community. This same grand jury report implied that St. Augustine was "merely a symbol for the Negro civil rights movement" rather than admitting to any ingrained problems.[241]

As would be expected, the SCLC declined these terms, with King arguing that they asked for "the Negro community to give all and the white community to give nothing." Robert Hayling, the local resident who might know best, added that the report was "based on the false assumption that St. Augustine had genuinely peaceful race relations until the Southern Christian Leadership Conference 'picked' it as a symbol before the world."[242]

King and Hayling were attempting to keep pressure on White politicians. The civil rights bill had not passed yet, and St. Augustine offered the opportunity to keep segregation and oppression in the news. In fact, not only did the SCLC decline the grand jury recommendation, but they also planned for additional demonstrations as a way to lessen the impact of the recommendations. On June 19, protests continued, with lunch counter sit-ins and an organized wade-in at the White beach.[243]

The evening of June 18 erupted as KKK leaders J.B. Stoner, Don Cochran and Al Massey spoke to a group of approximately one thousand White citizens in the Plaza area. Violence on a limited basis occurred as law enforcement worked to keep the sides separated.

This escalation of marching and violence led Mayor Shelley, state senator Pope and other community leaders to call Governor Bryant and ask him to issue an executive order banning further night marches in the city. Bryant, a known segregationist, agreed, stating that both segregationists and anti-segregationists were guilty of "certain lawlessness and utter disregard for the laws of Florida." Despite grumbling from both camps, both complied with the order, and on June 19, there was a general calmness to the evening.[244]

Wade-ins at the beach continued, with June 22 being a major struggle for all involved. Nineteen protestors attempted to enter the surf and were attacked by Klan members and local segregationists. Dozens of law enforcement officers responded to the situation. Six members of the Klan were arrested that afternoon, while a cameraman from Denmark was injured.[245]

June 1964 saw the use of "wade-in" protests in an attempt to integrate segregated St. Augustine beaches. African Americans wanting to visit the beach had previously been required to travel south of St. Augustine to Butler Beach, one of many "black beaches" in the state in the days of segregation. *Image courtesy State Archives of Florida.*

Florida governor LeRoy Collins, shown shaking hands with President Lyndon B. Johnson, was in attendance on July 2, 1964, when Johnson signed the Civil Rights Act of 1964. This act essentially outlawed segregation and ended employment discrimination based on race, sex, religion and national origin. *Image courtesy State Archives of Florida.*

On July 2, 1964, President Lyndon B. Johnson signed the Civil Rights Act of 1964 into law. In short, this legislation ended segregation in public places while also banning employment discrimination based on race, color, religion, sex or national origin. The efforts of Black residents of St. Augustine in keeping pressure on the national media and politicians cannot be overstated.

Despite joyous celebrations, the work in St. Augustine was far from finished. On July 4, Independence Day, over 60 robed Klan members descended on the Plaza, followed by 150 supporters, to voice their disagreement with the act. Led by Klan leaders J.B. Stoner, Connie Lynch and Hoss Manucy, the crowd was worked into a frenzy and marched in front of businesses that had desegregated. Among those was James Brock's Monson Motor Lodge. Marchers carried signs with vile language.[246]

When Brock asked Stoner why the Monson had been singled out, Stoner replied, "We're just trying to help you get some _____ business." On the

This page: With the Civil Rights Act signed, King and others left St. Augustine. Despite continued hardships for African American residents, the 1965 quadricentennial went off as planned, featuring dancers, music, plays and other entertainment. Visiting dignitaries would see only the best St. Augustine could offer during their visits. *Images courtesy State Archives of Florida.*

advice of another motel owner, Brock reinstituted segregation at his hotel, encountering the wrath of Judge Bryan Simpson, who ordered Brock serve Blacks or risk fines up to $1,000 per day.[247]

Pro-segregation pickets were not the only method used by the Klan and others to protest the newly adopted law. Businesses complying with the Civil Rights Act were subject to violence, including Molotov cocktails being hurled through windows. Black residents who risked acting on their new freedoms were subject to violent beatings. Many local Black residents began to turn on the SCLC and Martin Luther King Jr. as having used them and their city to further efforts to pass civil rights legislation. With Dr. King gone, the press also left, leaving local Black residents to face the wrath of angry Whites.[248]

In September 1965, the quadricentennial festivities went off as planned. Dignitaries including Count Alvaro Armada of Spain, a direct descendant of Pedro Menéndez de Aviles, cut the gigantic birthday cake. Visitors enjoyed music, dancing, costumed performances and lectures from historians. A Pan American Center, located on St. George Street, was dedicated. Here was featured an exhibit of modern Latin American art and historically based exhibits.[249]

Quadricentennial events were highlighted in many papers throughout the United States. Broadcasts were sent to Latin America. The overall event was celebrated "for affirming the connections between Europe and the United States and for demonstrating that the Spanish heritage of the United States 'can never be annihilated by changing the soil.'"[250]

And what of the Monson Motor Lodge? Demands of tourists have changed dramatically since the 1960s. By the beginning of the twenty-first century, the Monson, renamed the Monson Riverfront Inn, was seen by many as a relic of a bygone day. Despite the historic significance of the structure, owner Kanti Patel demolished the Monson in 2003 to make way for the "Hilton St. Augustine Historic Bayfront." Salvaged from the true "historic" site are steps that led to the swimming pool. Small plaques acknowledging these steps and the role played by Jewish clergy during the events of 1964 can be found if one looks hard enough. James Brock, the Monson Motor Lodge owner at the forefront of much controversy in 1964, died on September 11, 2007. His remains are buried in Evergreen Cemetery in St. Augustine.[251]

Chapter 5

WOMEN ARE NOT DISASTERS

Roxcy O'Neal Bolton and Her Struggle for Women's Equality

Your colossal gall is exceeded only by my tolerance, despite the stress upon my good nature.

In response to your letter of October 26, 1971, to make available your facilities for the meetings and conventions, it would seem that your common sense would tell you that a feminist, committed to equality for all women, would not be caught dead in that establishment of yours that exploits, degrades, uses and abuses the bodies of women. I can think of no place so objectionable, so oppressive to all womankind as yours.

So wrote Roxcy O'Neal Bolton in a reply to Thomas V. Zemsta, the assistant director of sales for the Playboy Plaza Hotel located in Miami Beach, in November 1971, after receiving a packet of promotional materials advertising the hotel as a space for meetings and conferences. Less than a week later, Bolton received a reply confirming that the Playboy Plaza Hotel had removed her name from its mailing list.[252]

In a life that lasted ninety years, Roxcy O'Neal Bolton was a champion for the equality of women, often leading the fight against long-ingrained traditions while still being able to embrace the traditions of motherhood and being a wife. She also served as a leader in the crusade to bring the issue of violence against women to the forefront.

Bolton was born on June 3, 1926, in the town of Duck Hill, Mississippi, located in Montgomery County. Duck Hill is a town of only around 1,500, and it had only around 550 residents when Roxcy was born. The town of

Duck Hill was named after a Choctaw chief and medicine man. A statue memorializes Chief Duck alongside Route 51 in the town.

Life was difficult in the small town. Roxcy's father was a farmer and her mother a schoolteacher. She was one of ten children and one of only three to live past infancy. While still in elementary school, young Roxcy decided she wanted to be a member of Congress. "Sometimes on the way to school the bridges would be washed out. I wanted to be a congressman so I could build bridges."[253]

It was in April 1937 that the ten-year-old Roxcy witnessed something that would change her worldview forever. On April 13, 1937, Roxcy, along with a large percentage of those from Duck Hill, witnessed the lynching of two African American males.

On December 30, 1936, George Sam Windham, a local grocer, was shot dead through the store's front window screen. The

In a life spanning ninety years, Roxcy O'Neal Bolton served as a voice for those who often did not have one of their own. Her efforts on behalf of sexual abuse victims had a lasting effect on how these crimes were treated by law enforcement and medical staff. *Image courtesy State Archives of Florida.*

sheriff said that in addition to the murder, the assailant had ransacked the store. Stories circulated that an amount between $200 and $350 was missing from the cash register, depending on the report. Sheriff Edgar Wright arrested three brothers, Alvie, T.L. and Elijah Dorrah, along with Joe Ed McDaniels soon after the murder. All four maintained their innocence, and Sheriff Wright stated there were other suspects.

On January 19, 1937, police charged Roosevelt Townes, a twenty-five-year-old African American, with the murder of George Windham. Townes and his wife were sharecroppers who aroused the suspicion of a local by the name of Mr. Prestage, who claimed that Townes had a large amount of cash on him. When questioned, Townes fled the area, becoming a highly wanted fugitive; a $500 cash reward was placed on his head.

In April, Roosevelt Townes was arrested in Memphis, Tennessee. Townes appeared in Memphis court on April 5, 1937, and was released to the Jackson County police department and Sheriff Wright. An acquaintance of Townes, Robert "Bootjack" McDaniels, was also accused and arrested.

On April 13, the accused were brought to court by Wright and several of his deputies. With the assistance of their court-appointed attorneys, both men pleaded not guilty. During a lunch recess, Sheriff Wright was escorting the prisoners back to jail when a mob of approximately one hundred White men overpowered Wright and his deputies. The officers put up little resistance and did not draw their weapons. They later claimed not to have recognized any members of the mob.

The mob loaded Townes and McDaniels on a school bus and drove the prisoners out of town. Reports stated a line of forty cars followed the bus. The White men chained Townes and McDaniels together. When they arrived at their destination, an estimated crowd of five hundred was waiting. Members of the mob shackled Townes and McDaniels to trees and tortured them until they confessed to the crime. The White mob shot and killed McDaniels before piling brush around the trees, dousing it and the men with gasoline and lighting them on fire. The death certificate for Roosevelt Townes states he was "burned to a crisp."[254]

As was the case in many racially motivated crimes of the era, there were no arrests made. Relaying the views of most citizens, the *Enterprise-Tocsin* newspaper stated:

> *We do not condone lynchings, but if two persons ever deserved lynching the two brutes at Duck Hill richly deserved what they got. We have no sympathy to waste on them, none whatsoever. Nothing will ever come from any investigation the Governor or anybody else will make, and no one member of the mob will ever be arrested. Even should some arrests be made there is not a jury in Mississippi that would ever convict any mob member. That is a fact and everyone knows it.*[255]

In a memorial article, the *Miami Herald* quoted Roxcy's son, David: "That may have been the catalyst for a lot of the things Roxcy did in the future. That affected her."[256]

After high school, Roxcy started what many considered a normal life for a young woman at the time. She left home and moved to Miami, where she found an office job and joined the Young Democrats. Soon she was married, had a son and divorced. She would later remarry, have three more children and be divorced a second time.

From her arrival in Miami, Roxcy became a forceful voice for the underrepresented: women, African Americans and those who did not feel they had a voice. She became their voice while helping them find theirs.

With the founding of the National Organization of Women (NOW) in 1966, Bolton became one of the first members from the state of Florida.

Roxcy O'Neal Bolton with her second husband, David Bolton, a United States Navy officer. David would later serve as president of Men for ERA. *Image courtesy State Archives of Florida.*

Soon, Bolton was elected to the national board of directors, where she served as vice president. Bolton has been credited with the 1968 founding of the local Miami-Dade chapter of the organization, serving as its first president. The new political power she had acquired led her to be able to persuade Indiana senator Birch Bayh to hold hearings on a controversial new bill, the Equal Rights Amendment. While the amendment was able to pass through the United States Congress, it did not pass in enough states and to this day is not a part of the Constitution. This failure chewed at Roxcy for the rest of her life.

By the mid-1970s, however, Bolton had left NOW. Author Meeghan Kane states that Bolton felt the group was struggling in trying to take on too many issues, all to the detriment of what Bolton considered the primary goal, passage of the Equal Rights Amendment. Scholar Laura E. Brock stated that Bolton "quit the organization in 1976 over what she viewed as the denigration of motherhood by the group." In May 1977, the *Miami Herald* quoted Bolton: "Some of the liberated women are all balled up. They forget their responsibilities to family and children. I believe you accept new roles, but you don't abandon the old ones. Our children are tomorrow's world." Whatever Bolton's reason for leaving NOW, her days as a crusader had not ended.[257]

Roxcy Bolton was not one to take no for an answer, and when she took up a cause, she seldom lost. One of her earliest triumphs was something we take for granted today. Women were not able to eat in the same dining room with men at several Miami department store restaurants. As Bolton recalls:

> *I went shopping at Burdines Department Store in Miami with my little babies. I dashed upstairs to get a bit of lunch. It was just rush, rush when you had little children. A long line of women waited for a table while the men's section had empty tables. No men were standing in line! That really pissed me off as I stood in line, anxious, impatient, and aggravated. At home, I called the store's vice president in charge of personnel. "This separate seating for men and women is intolerable. I want to talk to you about it." We set up a meeting….*
>
> *He invited us into his office and I wasted no time. "We are here to change the policy of seating."*
>
> *He was incredulous. "But Mrs. Bolton, we have done this for so long!"*
>
> *I wouldn't budge. "I am telling you that people will like the change. You have 30 days…or I will stand in front of your store and pass out the best tuna sandwiches in town and boycott people from eating in your restaurant*

since you don't let women have the same privileges as men." I could tell by his body language that it concerned him. "Within 30 days of today, I want a letter stating you will not continue the policy of seating men and making women stand in line. Men and women sleep together, why can't they eat together."

Within 30 days I received the letter.

Following the meeting with Burdines, the same thing happened at Jordan Marsh Department Store. After they sent a letter stating their change in policy, I went to lunch with my husband to check it out. When the dining room receptionist greeted us, I asked, "What happened? You don't have a men's dining room anymore?"

She said, "No, the government made us change it."...

I'm sure that was the story Jordan Marsh told their employees. They didn't want to say feminists made them change.

We made a difference....We made it better.[258]

Roxcy O'Neal Bolton, seen carrying a child, along with Representative Gwen Cherry (*left, wearing white pants*), led a march in favor of Florida ratifying the Equal Rights Amendment. Failing to pass the ERA was something that bothered Bolton throughout her life. *Image courtesy State Archives of Florida.*

Bolton had a big hand in changing something that we are familiar with on a yearly basis: the naming of hurricanes. "Hurricanes are disasters, destroying life and communities and leaving a lasting and devastating effect on those affected. Women are human beings and deeply resent being arbitrarily associated with disaster," she stated, explaining why the cause was so important to her and other women.[259]

Beginning in 1953, tropical storms and hurricanes received female names. Seeing the injustice in women's names being used exclusively for potentially cataclysmic events, Bolton stated to the press in 1970, "I'm sick and tired of hearing that 'Cheryl was no lady and she devastated such and such town' or 'Betsy annihilated this or that.'"[260]

Staff of the National Weather Service met Bolton's first attempts at changing hurricane names with derisive scoffs and laughter. The National Hurricane Center attempted to push off the issue, claiming that the mail it received was in favor of using women's names for hurricanes by a margin of eight or nine to one. Bolton shot back, "As long as people can name [hurricanes] after us it's just another way of putting women down....In 1970 it is time to take women seriously as human beings."[261]

In a sarcastic effort, Bolton urged that tropical storms and hurricanes be named after United States senators, her reason being that these politicians "delight in having streets, bridges, buildings—especially Federal buildings—named for them, as well as parks, dams, forests, waterways, clubs…just about anything before the public." Dr. Karl Johanssen, then the associate director of the National Hurricane Center, replied asking if it was her intention to "cast a slur on U.S. Senators?" Seldom unprepared, Bolton retorted, "You don't mind degrading and humiliating women, but you're reluctant about senators?"

Bolton tried again later, suggesting storms be named after birds. Johanssen declined this naming convention out of hand, as it might offend members of the Audubon Society. In a letter to the National Weather Service, Bolton accused the National Hurricane Center of showing more concern "about the Audubon Society and regard for birds—but not for women."[262]

The sustained pressure from women's groups, however, finally led to a change in naming protocol in 1979. Male names that year included Bob, David, Frederic and Henri. Since 1979, the National Weather Service has used women's and men's names alternately for storms, with the naming schedule published in advance. After a period of six years, a name may be repeated. Devastating storms often have their names retired.[263]

While these larger, more well-known exploits kept Roxcy's name in the papers, and on the minds of elected officials, she felt affinity for, and a need to help, the unprotected, the unnamed and the persecuted.

Sitting in her Miami home, Bolton received an impassioned phone call that police were arresting women for breastfeeding their babies in a local park. She immediately called the office of then state attorney general Bob Shevin. Shevin was a Democrat who had formerly served in the state house of representatives before his election as attorney general in 1970. Aides called Shevin from a meeting to take the call from the enraged Bolton, who began her plea with the question, "Did your mother breastfeed you?" Shevin was none too happy about having been required to take the call, but Bolton won the day. Shevin called both the Miami mayor and the city attorney. This call helped avert what could have become a larger crisis.[264]

Perhaps Bolton's most important role, however, was in engaging the Miami police force to more professionally and courteously deal with women who brought forth allegations of sexual abuse. Bolton had seen how authorities treated these women and successfully argued that victims were discouraged from reporting crimes due to the treatment by law enforcement.

Her work with victims coupled with the slow rate of change led Bolton to organize the Protest March Against Crimes of Rape, held on October 4, 1971. Protestors' demands included more foot patrols on Miami streets, better street lighting and a hotline number to report serious crimes. If a female called to report sexual abuse, a female officer received the call, and any interviews with female victim had to have a female office present.

In 1972, Bolton founded Women in Distress, the first women's rescue shelter in Florida. The shelter provided temporary lodging, counseling, legal advice and assistance, along with a support system for those with substance addictions.[265]

The struggle continued into 1973, when Bolton announced her proposal for the creation of a sexual abuse treatment center at Jackson Memorial Hospital in Miami. Her dream became reality in January 1974 with the opening of a twenty-four-hour treatment center. Bolton requested that victims be taken here first rather than being immediately questioned by law enforcement. She firmly believed that having a center such as this would encourage victims to seek treatment. She was correct. Within the first six months of service, more than three hundred victims, ages eight to seventy-four, had been attended to.

Patients received specialized care at the center. It became a one-stop location, with physical exams, counselling, labs and law enforcement services. As the

In 1974, at the leadership of Bolton (*right*), the Rape Crisis Center was opened at Jackson Memorial Hospital in Miami. This center provided specialized care and allowed victims a safe environment away from traditional emergency room facilities. *Image courtesy State Archives of Florida.*

center was a part of the hospital, these services were provided separately from traditional emergency room and treatment facilities. These efforts were made in order not to stigmatize victims but rather give them privacy and personalized care. It is also important to note that staff were both female and male. Center director Dr. Dorothy Hicks and her staff felt that isolating victims from males provided the message that all men were bad.[266]

As Roxcy grew older, her accomplishments began to receive significantly more public recognition. In 1984, she was elected to the Florida Women's Hall of Fame. In 1992, she helped found and open the Women's Park in Miami. This fifteen-acre park includes a playground for children, a picnic pavilion, public art displays and the Roxcy O'Neal Bolton Women's History Gallery. In 1993, the rape treatment center she helped found was renamed the Roxcy Bolton Rape Treatment Center. The National Women's History Project recognized Bolton in 2014 as one of the National Women's History Month honorees. Later that year, the Miami Women's Club recognized Roxcy for being a "leading force of the women's rights movement in Miami."[267]

Toward the end of Bolton's life, health issues slowed her considerably, something that politicians were never able to do. When asked why she did not go into politics herself, she stated, with her usual sharp wit, "I didn't have the patience. My interests are women, employee, and black rights. I couldn't listen to some zoning lawyer tell a bunch of lies or to some damn fool thing that's not good for the city. I am not suited to be a public official."[268]

Bolton passed away on May 17, 2017, in Coral Gables, Florida; her remains are buried in Old Miami Cemetery.

Although she was often at odds with governmental bodies, praise for Bolton came from many public servants in the wake of her death. Former Coral Gables city mayor Jim Cason stated,

Bolton was an inveterate fighter for human rights, for women's rights, for African Americans, for gays, for the dispossessed. She was a good check on city government for all the years, making sure that people did the right thing from her point of view. She was just a scrapper and a fighter through her whole life. She was refreshing, a terror in her time, and every community needs someone like a Roxcy Bolton to push back and make sure people are doing the right thing.[269]

The concise words of then Coral Gables city manager Cathy Swanson-Rivenback perhaps best sum up what Roxcy O'Neal Bolton accomplished: "Our community and our country are better for her tireless advocacy."[270]

NOTES

Introduction

1. Legal Information Institute, "Civil Rights."
2. Stanford Encyclopedia of Philosophy, "Human Rights."

Chapter 1

3. "Fla Gals May Vote"; National Archives, "19th Amendment."
4. Johnson, "Kate Gordon," 365.
5. Ibid., 365–66.
6. Ibid., 366; Center for American Women and Politics, "Teach a Girl to Lead."
7. Quoted in Taylor, "Woman Suffrage Movement," 42–43.
8. Ibid., 43.
9. Burnett-Haney, "Florida," 577–80.
10. Taylor, "Woman Suffrage Movement," 44.
11. Quoted in "Why Southern Women Desire," 26.
12. Van Howe, "Women's Suffrage Movement," 37–38.
13. Ibid., 38.
14. Burnett-Haney, "Florida," 577–80; Taylor, "Woman Suffrage Movement," 44.
15. Taylor, "Woman Suffrage Movement," 44–45.
16. Johnson, "Florida Women," 299; League of Women Voters Pensacola Bay Area, *When Women Vote*, 6; Taylor, "Woman Suffrage Movement," 46.
17. Taylor, "Woman Suffrage Movement," 47.
18. League of Women Voters Pensacola Bay Area, *When Women Vote*, 7.

19. Ibid., 8.
20. Ibid., 8.
21. Taylor, "Woman Suffrage Movement," 48–49; readers are also referred to Johnson, "Kate Gordon."
22. Taylor, "Woman Suffrage Movement," 50.
23. Ibid., 49–50.
24. Ibid., 50–51.
25. Ibid., 52.
26. Ibid., 53.
27. "41 Women Arrested."
28. "Suffs Sentenced."
29. Taylor, "Woman Suffrage Movement," 53–54.
30. "Florida Women Demand."
31. "Branch of Equal Suffrage League."
32. "Noted Suffrage Leader."
33. Taylor, "Woman Suffrage Movement," 54–55.
34. Ibid., 56; Votapka, *Fellsmere Firsts*.
35. Votapka, *Fellsmere Firsts*.
36. Taylor, "Woman Suffrage Movement," 56–58.
37. Ibid., 58.
38. Johnson, "Florida Women," 301–3.
39. Ibid., 304–5; "Catts Urges Florida."
40. "Florida Women," 307; League of Women Voters Pensacola Bay Area, *When Women Vote*, 34–35.
41. Johnson, "Florida Women," 307; League of Women Voters Pensacola Bay Area. *When Women Vote*, 35–36.
42. Johnson, "Florida Women," 311–12; University of California, Berkeley, "19th Amendment."
43. "Fla Gals May Vote"; Johnson, "Florida Women," 305.

Chapter 2

44. Lamb, *Blackout*, 24.
45. Ibid., 7.
46. Quoted in Lamb, *Blackout*, 34.
47. Ibid., 31–32.
48. Robinson and Duckett, *Never Had It Made*, 30–35.
49. Quoted in Lamb, *Blackout*, 8.
50. Robinson and Duckett, *Never Had It Made*, 35.
51. "'Guess I'm Just a Guinea Pig.'"
52. Lamb, *Blackout*, 46–47.

53. Ibid., 48.

54. Quoted in Lamb, *Blackout*, 48.

55. Quoted in Lamb, *Blackout*, 47.

56. Lamb, *Blackout*, 49–50.

57. Ibid., 50–51.

58. Ibid., 50–52; "Montreal Puts Negro Player."

59. "'Guess I'm Just a Guinea Pig'"; Lamb, *Blackout*, 51.

60. See *Daytona Beach Morning Journal*, October 24, 25 and 26, 1945.

61. "Jackie Robinson Joins Montreal."

62. Robinson and Duckett, *Never Had It Made*, 40–41.

63. Quoted in Falkner, *Great Time Coming*, 128.

64. Lamb, *Blackout*, 69.

65. Lamb, *Blackout*, 66–67; Robinson and Duckett, *Never Had It Made*, 44.

66. Lamb, *Blackout*, 83–86.

67. Falkner, *Great Time Coming*, 130–31; Lamb, *Blackout*, 88.

68. Lamb, *Blackout*, 90–91.

69. Lamb, "'Fine Line' Still Segregates"; Lamb, *Blackout*, 92.

70. Lamb, *Blackout*, 92–93.

71. Quoted in Lamb, *Blackout*, 94–95.

72. Ibid., 95; Robinson and Smith, *My Own Story*, 77.

73. Robinson and Duckett, *Never Had It Made*, 44–45.

74. Baseball Reference, "Lou Rochelli."

75. Lamb, *Blackout*, 100.

76. Robinson and Smith, *My Own Story*, 77.

77. Robinson and Duckett, *Never Had It Made*, 45–46.

78. Lamb, *Blackout*, 104–105; Rampersad, *Jackie Robinson*, 145–47; Robinson and Duckett, *Never Had It Made*, 45–46.

79. Lamb, *Blackout*, 106; Robinson and Duckett, *Never Had It Made*, 45.

80. "Walker's Bat Ices."

81. Lamb, *Blackout*, 108.

82. Ibid., 110–12.

83. Quoted in Lamb, *Blackout*, 113–14.

84. Baseball Reference, "Spider Jorgensen."

85. See Lamb, *Blackout*, 124–25 for Mexican League efforts to sign American baseball players.

86. Lamb, *Blackout*, 135.

87. Ibid., 135–36; "Montreal Game."

88. Lamb, *Blackout*, 140–142; Falkner, *Great Time Coming*, 133.

89. Lamb, *Blackout*, 142.

90. Ibid., 142–43.

91. Ibid., 142.

92. Ibid., 151.
93. Ibid., 152.
94. Lamb, *Blackout*, 163; Rampersad, *Jackie Robinson*, 148.
95. Lamb, *Blackout*, 163–64.
96. Ibid., 164.
97. Ibid., 164.
98. Ibid., 171–72.
99. Baseball Reference, "Jackie Robinson."
100. Baseball Reference, "Johnny Wright."
101. Baseball Reference, "Jackie Robinson."
102. United States Department of the Interior National Park Service, "City Island Ball Park," section 7, page 1.
103. "Rachel Robinson."
104. Ibid. (all quotes).
105. "City Strips Official's Name."
106. City of Sanford, Florida, "City Commission Memorandum."
107. Ibid.

Chapter 3

108. Padgett, "C.K. Steele," 79; Rabby, *Pain and the Promise*, 28.
109. Smith and Killian, *Field Reports*, 3–4; Martin Luther King, Jr. Research and Education Institute, "Montgomery Bus Boycott."
110. Smith and Killian, *Field Reports*, 4.
111. United States Supreme Court, *"Brown v. Board of Education."*
112. Smith and Killian, *Field Reports*, 4–5.
113. Ibid., 5.
114. Ibid., 5.
115. Ibid., 5.
116. Ibid., 4–5.
117. Rabby, *Pain and the Promise*, 9; Smith and Killian, *Field Reports*, 7. It is worth noting some sources list the actions of students Jakes and Patterson as having occurred on May 26, while others use the date May 27. After review, I have selected May 26.
118. Steele, "Tallahassee Bus Protest Story."
119. Killian, "Organization, Rationality, and Spontaneity," 773.
120. Rabby, *Pain and the Promise*, 10–11.
121. Padgett, "Push for Equality," 16; Rabby, *Pain and the Promise*, 11–12; Smith and Killian, *Field Reports*, 7.
122. Rabby, *Pain and the Promise*, 11.
123. Ibid., 12–13.

124. Ibid., 12.

125. Killian, "Organization, Rationality, and Spontaneity," 774; Rabby, *Pain and the Promise*, 12–13; Smith, *Civil Rights Movement*, 31; Smith and Killian, *Field Reports*, 7.

126. Rabby, *Pain and the Promise*, 12; Smith and Killian, *Field Reports*, 34.

127. Rabby, *Pain and the Promise*, 13.

128. Martin Luther King, Jr. Research and Education Institute, "Supreme Court Affirms Flemming."

129. Padgett, "Push for Equality," 17; Rabby, *Pain and the Promise*, 13; Smith, *Civil Rights Movement*, 31–32; Smith and Killian, *Field Reports*, 8.

130. Rabby, *Pain and the Promise*, 14.

131. Ibid.

132. Padgett, "Push for Equality," 17; Rabby, *Pain and the Promise*, 14; Smith, *Civil Rights Movement*, 32; Smith and Killian, *Field Reports*, 8.

133. Padgett, "Push for Equality," 17; Rabby, *Pain and the Promise*, 15.

134. Killian, "Organization, Rationality, and Spontaneity," 774; Padgett, "C.K. Steele," 62; Rabby, *Pain and the Promise*, 15.

135. Padgett, "C.K. Steele," 62.

136. Rabby, *Pain and the Promise*, 17–18.

137. Padgett, "Push for Equality," 17.

138. Ibid.; Rabby, *Pain and the Promise*, 14–15; Smith, *Civil Rights Movement*, 33; Smith and Killian, *Field Reports*, 8.

139. Rabby, *Pain and the Promise*, 18; Smith and Killian, *Field Reports*, 8.

140. Rabby, *Pain and the Promise*, 18–19.

141. Padgett, "C.K. Steele," 65–66; Padgett, "Push for Equality," 19; Rabby, *Pain and the Promise*, 20–21; Smith and Killian, *Field Reports*, 8.

142. Steele, "Tallahassee Bus Protest Story."

143. Both quotes are found in Rabby, *Pain and the Promise*, 22.

144. Ibid., 23.

145. Padgett, "Push for Equality," 20; Rabby, *Pain and the Promise*, 27; Smith and Killian, *Field Reports*, 9.

146. Smith and Killian, *Field Reports*, 9–10.

147. Padgett, "C.K. Steele," 77; Rabby, *Pain and the Promise*, 18.

148. Padgett, "C.K. Steele," 72; Padgett, "Push for Equality," 20.

149. Rabby, *Pain and the Promise*, 33.

150. Ibid.; Smith and Killian, *Field Reports*, 10.

151. Rabby, *Pain and the Promise*, 36–37.

152. Padgett, "Push for Equality," 20–21; Rabby, *Pain and the Promise*, 43–44; Smith and Killian, *Field Reports*, 11–12.

153. Padgett, "Push for Equality," 20; Rabby, *Pain and the Promise*, 43–44; Smith, *Civil Rights Movement*, 99–100; Smith and Killian, *Field Reports*, 12; M.T. Weiss, "Weiss in Tallahassee."

154. Padgett, "Push for Equality," 21; Rabby, *Pain and the Promise*, 43–45; Smith, *Civil Rights Movement*, 101, Smith and Killian, *Field Reports*, 12, Weiss, "Weiss in Tallahassee."

155. Padgett, "C.K. Steele," 96.

156. Quoted in Padgett, "C.K. Steele," 106; see also Gilano, "Story of Tallahassee."

157. Martin Luther King, Jr. Research and Education Institute., "Montgomery Bus Boycott"; Rabby, *Pain and the Promise*, 45–46.

158. Rabby, *Pain and the Promise*, 47.

159. Ibid., 48.

160. Padgett, "C.K. Steele," 117–18; Rabby, *Pain and the Promise*, 48; Smith and Killian, *Field Reports*, 12–13.

161. Padgett, "C.K. Steele," 118; Rabby, *Pain and the Promise*, 48–49; Smith and Killian, *Field Reports*, 13.

162. Rabby, *Pain and the Promise*, 51; Smith and Killian, *Field Reports*, 13.

163. Padgett, "C.K. Steele," 122–23; Rabby, *Pain and the Promise*, 51–52; Smith, *Civil Rights Movement*, 102; Smith and Killian, *Field Reports*, 13.

164. Padgett, "C.K. Steele," 126–28; Rabby, *Pain and the Promise*, 54–55; Smith and Killian, *Field Reports*, 15.

165. Padgett, "C.K. Steele," 127–28; Rabby, *Pain and the Promise*. Readers are also directed to Spagna, *Test Ride*. This book is a daughter's attempt to find the truth about her deceased father's actions in Tallahassee in 1957.

166. Rabby, *Pain and the Promise*, 58.

167. Smith, *Civil Rights Movement*, 75, 103.

168. Carlisle and Carlisle, *Tallahassee in History*, 102; Tallahassee Arts Guide, "Civil Rights Heritage Walk."

Chapter 4

169. "Dr. King Describes."

170. Slate, "Florida Room," 541.

171. Colburn, *Racial Change*, 16.

172. Slate, "Florida Room," 542.

173. Colburn, "Push for Equality," 28.

174. Hillyer, "Cold War Conquistadors," 117.

175. Abernathy, *Walls Came Tumbling Down*, 282.

176. Hillyer, "Cold War Conquistadors," 137.

177. Colburn, *Racial Change*, 72.

178. Ibid., 58, 122.

179. Ibid., 30–32.

180. Ibid., 32.

181. Hillyer, "Cold War Conquistadors," 126.

182. Ibid., 138.

183. Colburn, *Racial Change*, 32–33; Slate, "Florida Room," 542.

184. Colburn, *Racial Change*, 33; Slate, "Florida Room," 542–43.

185. Colburn, *Racial Change*, 34.

186. Abernathy, *Walls Came Tumbling Down*, 283; Colburn, *Racial Change*, 34.

187. Colburn, *Racial Change*, 36–38.

188. Colburn, "Push for Equality," 26–27; Colburn, *Racial Change*, 36.

189. Colburn, *Racial Change*, 40–41.

190. Colburn, "Push for Equality," 27; Colburn, *Racial Change*, 40–42; Reider, *Can't Get No Satisfaction*, 97–98; Wikipedia, "James W. Kynes."

191. Colburn, *Racial Change*, 44.

192. Ibid., 48.

193. Ibid., 49.

194. Ibid., 51.

195. Colburn, *Racial Change*, 51–52; Slate, "Florida Room," 554.

196. Colburn, *Racial Change*, 52.

197. Ibid., 53.

198. Branch, *Pillar of Fire*, 141–43; Colburn, *Racial Change*, 53.

199. Civil Rights Library of St. Augustine, "Investigative Report"; Colburn, *Racial Change*, 54.

200. Colburn, *Racial Change*, 54–55.

201. Ibid., 55–60.

202. Abernathy, *Walls Came Tumbling Down*, 284.

203. Colburn, *Racial Change*, 62; Hillyer, "Cold War Conquistador," 138; Slate, "Florida Room," 543.

204. Colburn, *Racial Change*, 62–63.

205. Abernathy, *Walls Came Tumbling Down*, 284.

206. Colburn, "Push for Equality," 25; Slate, "Florida Room," 543.

207. Abernathy, *Walls Came Tumbling Down*, 294; Colburn, *Racial Change*, 63; Young, *Easy Burden*, 294.

208. Young, *Easy Burden*, 294.

209. Slate, "Florida Room," 544; Young, *Easy Burden*, 294.

210. Slate, "Florida Room," 545.

211. Colburn, *Racial Change*, 63–64.

212. Young, *Easy Burden*, 295.

213. Slate, "Florida Room," 544.

214. Colburn, *Racial Change*, 64.

215. Ibid., 65.

216. Branch, *Pillar of Fire*, 277.

217. Ibid., 239.

218. Ibid., 278.

219. Ibid.

220. Branch, *Pillar of Fire*, 278–84; Slate, "Florida Room," 551.

221. "88 More Seized"; Branch, *Pillar of Fire*, 278–79; Colburn, *Racial Change*, 66–67; Hillyer, "Cold War Conquistadors," 139; Warren, *Takes All Summer*, 73.

222. Branch, *Pillar of Fire*, 284–85; Colburn, *Racial Change*, 68–69; Reider, *Can't Get No Satisfaction*, 98.

223. Warren, *Takes All Summer*, 77–78.

224. Colburn, *Racial Change*, 91; "Martin Luther King and 17 Others"; Warren, *Takes All Summer*, 78.

225. Colburn, *Racial Change*, 91–92; "Martin Luther King and 17 Others"; Reider, *Can't Get No Satisfaction*, 110.

226. Branch, *Pillar of Fire*, 538–39; Colburn, *Racial Change*, 92; "Martin Luther King and 17 Others."

227. Branch, *Pillar of Fire*, 539; Colburn, *Racial Change*, 92; "Martin Luther King and 17 Others"; Reider, *Can't Get No Satisfaction*, 110.

228. Abernathy, *Walls Came Tumbling Down*, 288; Branch, *Pillar of Fire*, 339–40; Colburn, *Racial Change*, 92–93; "Martin Luther King and 17 Others."

229. Slate, "Florida Room," 561–62.

230. Branch, *Pillar of Fire*, 343; Reider, *Can't Get No Satisfaction*, 110–11.

231. Colburn, *Racial Change*, 99.

232. Abernathy, *Walls Came Tumbling Down*, 288–90.

233. Ibid., 289.

234. Ibid.

235. Colburn, *Racial Change*, 98–101.

236. Branch, *Pillar of Fire*, 354–55; Colburn, *Racial Change*, 99–100; Hillyer, "Cold War Conquistadors," 140; Reider, *Can't Get No Satisfaction*, 110–12; Slate, "Florida Room," 566.

237. Abernathy, *Walls Came Tumbling Down*, 289–90.

238. Ibid., 290; Branch, *Pillar of Fire*, 354–55; Colburn, *Racial Change*, 99–100; Hillyer, "Cold War Conquistadors," 140–41; Reider, *Can't Get No Satisfaction*, 111–12.

239. Colburn, *Racial Change*, 99.

240. Hillyer, "Cold War Conquistadors," 140.

241. Colburn, *Racial Change*, 100–101.

242. Ibid., 101.

243. Ibid., 103.

244. Ibid., 104–5.

245. Warren, *Takes All Summer*, 127–28.

246. Colburn, *Racial Change*, 111; Reider, *Can't Get No Satisfaction*, 113; Warren, *Takes All Summer*, 162.

247. Colburn, *Racial Change*, 111.

248. Ibid., 111–12; Reider, *Can't Get No Satisfaction*, 113–14; Warren, *Takes All Summer*, 165–66.

249. Hillyer, "Cold War Conquistadors," 152–53.

250. Ibid., 153.

251. "Demolition Begins."

Chapter 5

252. Florida Memory, "Handwritten Letter."

253. Roberts, "Roxcy Bolton."

254. *This Cruel War*, "Anniversary of Duck Hill."

255. "Just Saving the Costs."

256. Cohen, Fichtner and Brecher, "Civic Activist, Feminist, Trailblazer."

257. Brock, "Religion, Sex & Politics," 136; Cohen, Fichtner and Brecher, "Civic Activist, Feminist, Trailblazer"; Voss, "Roxcy Bolton."

258. Florida Memory, "Letter from Vice President."

259. Florida Memory, "What's in a Hurricane's Name?"; Roberts, "Roxcy Bolton."

260. Florida Memory, "What's in a Hurricane's Name?"

261. Ibid.

262. Ibid.; Hand and Savas, *Women of True Grit*, 156.

263. Florida Memory, "What's in a Hurricane's Name."

264. Harkas, "Woman's Place"; Voss, "Roxcy Bolton."

265. Harkas, "Roxcy's Heritage."

266. Florida Memory, "Roxcy Bolton."

267. Cohen, Fichtner and Brecher, "Civic Activist, Feminist, Trailblazer."

268. Hand and Savas, *Women of True Grit*, 156.

269. Cohen, Fichtner and Brecher, "Civic Activist, Feminist, Trailblazer."

270. Ibid.

BIBLIOGRAPHY

Articles

Brock, Laura E. "Religion and Women's Rights in Florida: An Examination of the Equal Rights Amendment Legislative Debates, 1972–1982." *Florida Historical Quarterly* 94 (Summer 2015): 1–39.

Cohen, Howard, Margarita Fichtner and Elinor Brecher. "Civic Activist, Feminist, Trailblazer Roxcy Bolton Dies at 90." *Miami Herald*, May 17, 2017.

Colburn, David R. "The Push for Equality: St. Augustine 1964." *Forum: Magazine of the Florida Humanities* 18 (Winter 1994/1995): 22–30.

Cooper, Algia R. "Brown V. Board of Education and Virgil Darnell Hawkins Twenty-Eight Years and Six Petitions to Justice." *Journal of Negro History* 64 (Winter 1979): 1–20.

Daytona Beach Evening Journal. "City Strips Official's Name from Park." August 12, 2020.

———. "Jackie Robinson: A Hero Remembered." September 16, 1990.

———. "Montreal Game at Jax Sunday Is Called Off." March 23, 1946.

———. "Montreal Sculptor Says He Improved on His Original Jackie Robinson Statue." September 15, 1990.

———. "Robinson, Wright Check in at Sanford." March 5, 1946.

———. "Walker's Bat Ices Dodgers' Win; Robinson Plays." March 18, 1946.

Daytona Beach Evening News. "Fla Gals May Vote at Last!" May 16, 1969. National Archives.

Daytona Beach News Journal. "Negro Beach Community Is in Development." August 28, 1949.

———. "Rachel Robinson: 'I Love the Statue.'" September 15, 1990.

Daytona Morning Journal. "Branch of Equal Suffrage League Formed." November 23, 1918.

———. "Catts Urges Florida Take Lead Support of Suffrage." June 6, 1919.

———. "Florida Women Demand Immediate Right to Serve on School Boards and Equal Suffrage in Daytona." September 19, 1918.

———. "Noted Suffrage Leader Will Address F.F.W. Clubs Tonight." November 22, 1918.

DeLand Sun News. "Jackie Robinson Joins Montreal at Daytona Beach." October 24, 1945.

———. "Negro Is Signed by Brooklyn Club." October 24, 1945.

Dickinson, Joy Wallace. "A Century Ago, Orlando Women's Bid to Vote Caused Shock and Jokes." *Orlando Sentinel*, October 14, 2012.

Elliott, I.W. "Protest in Tallahassee." *New Republic: A Journal of Opinion*, August 30, 1956, 3, 23.

Ensley, Gerald. "Daughter Recalls Father's Role in Tallahassee Bus Protest." *Tallahassee Democrat*, May 24, 2016. https://www.tallahassee.com/story/news/2016/05/24/fathers-courage-his-daughers-legacy-joe-spagna-tallahassee-bus-boycott/84785986/.

———. "The Ride to Equality Started 60 Years Ago." *Tallahassee Democrat*, May 20, 2016. https://www.tallahassee.com/story/news/2016/05/20/bus-boycott-60-years-later/84546580/.

Enterprise-Tocsin. "Just Saving the Costs of Court." April 22, 1937.

Florida Memory. "Roxcy Bolton: Advocate for Women in Crisis." *Floridiana*, 2017. https://www.floridamemory.com/items/show/332823.

———. "What's in a Hurricane's Name?" *Floridiana*, 2016. https://www.floridamemory.com/items/show/322857.

Gilano, Henry. "The Story of Tallahassee." *Militant* 20 (October 22, 1956).

Harkas, Margo. "Roxcy's Heritage." *Sun Sentinel*, May 26, 1999.

———. "A Woman's Place." *Sun Sentinel*, July 15, 1992.

Hillyer, Reiko. "Cold War Conquistadors: The St. Augustine Quadricentennial, Pan-Americanism, and the Civil Rights Movement in the Ancient City." *Journal of Southern History* 81 (February 2015): 117–56.

Hometown News. "Dr. Mary McLeod Bethune Statue Finally Unveiled." October 15, 2021.

Johnson, Kenneth R. "Florida Women Get the Vote." *Florida Historical Quarterly* 48 (January 1970): 299–312.

———. "Kate Gordon and the Woman-Suffrage Movement in the South." *Journal of Southern History* 38 (August 1972): 365–92.

Keen, Meeghan. "Roxcy O'Neal Bolton: Florida's Feminist Pioneer." *Unsweetened Magazine*, August 26, 2015.

Killian, Lewis M. "Organization, Rationality, and Spontaneity in the Civil Rights Movement." *American Sociological Review* 49 (December 1984): 770–83.

Killian, Lewis M., and Charles U. Smith. "Protest Leaders in a Southern Community." *Social Forces* 38 (March 1960): 253–57.

Lamb, Chris. "'Fine Line' Still Segregates Residential Neighborhoods." *Daytona Beach News Journal*, October 21, 1991.

———. "'What's Wrong with Baseball': The *Pittsburgh Courier* and the Beginning of Its Campaign to Integrate the National Pastime." *Western Journal of Black Studies* 26 (Winter 2002): 189–92.

Lamb, Chris, and Glen Bleske. "Democracy on the Field: The Black Press Takes on White Baseball." *Journalism History* 24 (Summer 1998): 51–59.

Lempel, Leonard. "The Immortal Mary McLeod Bethune." *Halifax Herald* 39 (Summer 2021): 6–15.

Mohl, Raymond A. "'South of the South?' Jews, Blacks, and the Civil Rights Movement in Miami, 1945–1960." *Journal of American Ethnic History* 18 (Winter 1999): 3–36.

Morris, Allen. "Florida's First Women Candidates." *Florida Historical Quarterly* 63, no. 4 (1984): 406–22.

Nelson, Gary. "Florida's Pioneer Feminist Roxcy Bolton Has Died." CBS News Miami, May 17, 2017. https://miami.cbslocal.com/2017/05/17/florida-feminist-roxcy-bolton/.

New York Times. "Dr. King Describes St. Augustine as Most Lawless City He's Seen; Reports Threats on His Life in Florida—Shots Are Fired into a Negro Automobile." June 6, 1964.

———. "88 More Seized in St. Augustine; Yale Chaplain Among Them—Mrs. Peabody Cheerful." April 2, 1964.

———. "Martin Luther King and 17 Others Jailed Trying to Integrate St. Augustine Restaurant." June 12, 1964.

Padgett, Gregory B. "The Push for Equality: A Bus Boycott Takes Root and Blossoms." *Forum: Magazine of the Florida Humanities* 18 (Winter 1994/1995):14–21.

Patterson, Gordon. "Ditches and Dreams: Nelson Fell and the Rise of Fellsmere." *Florida Historical Quarterly* 76 (Summer 1997): 1–19.

Redd, Kenny. "Suffrage: Long Road for Florida Women." *Panama City News*, June 19, 2020.

Roberts, Sam. "Roxcy Bolton, Feminist Crusader for Equality, Including in Naming Hurricanes, Dies at 90." *New York Times*, May 21, 2017.

Rose, Chanelle N. "Tourism and the Hispanicization of Race in Jim Crow Miami, 1945–1965." *Journal of Social History* 45 (2012): 735–56.

Sandusky Star Journal. "Suffs Sentenced, Six Days to Six Months." November 14, 1917.

Slate, Claudia S. "Florida Room: Battle for St. Augustine 1964: Public Record and Personal Recollection." *Florida Historical Quarterly* 84 (Spring 2006): 541–68.

Sporting News. "'Guess I'm Just a Guinea Pig' Says Jack Robinson; Realizes His Responsibilities in Montreal Tryout." November 1, 1945.

————. "Montreal Puts Negro Player on Spot." November 1, 1945.

St. Augustine Record. "Demolition Begins on Monson Inn." March 18, 2003.

Sunday News Journal. "Montreal Treats Players Fairly." March 10, 1946.

Syracuse Herald. "41 Women Arrested at White House." November 11, 1917.

Taylor, A. Elizabeth. "The Woman Suffrage Movement in Florida." *Florida Historical Quarterly* 36 (July 1957): 42–60.

Van Howe, Annette. "The Women's Suffrage Movement in Broward County and Florida." *Broward Legacy* (Summer/Fall 1991): 37–42.

Voss, Kimberly Wilmot. "The Florida Fight for Equality: The Equal Rights Amendment, Senator Lori Wilson and Mediated Catfights in the 1970s." *Florida Historical Quarterly* 88 (Fall 2009): 173–208.

————. "Roxcy Bolton: Tireless Feminist Organizer." *Ms. Magazine,* March 17, 2015. https://msmagazine.com/2015/03/17/roxcy-bolton-tireless-feminist-organizer/.

Weiss, Myra Tanner. "Weiss in Tallahassee Blasts Jim-Crow Trial: SWP Vice-Presidential Nominee Reports from Buse Case Court Room." *Militant* 20 (October 22, 1956): 1, 4.

Wilkinson, Francis. "The Forgotten History of America's Black Beach Resorts." Bloomberg, August 8, 2021. https://www.bloomberg.com/opinion/articles/2021-08-08/the-forgotten-history-of-america-s-black-beach-resorts.

Woman's Journal. "Why Southern Women Desire the Ballot." January 26, 1895.

Books

Abernathy, Ralph David. *And the Walls Came Tumbling Down.* New York: Harper & Row, 1989.

Altenese, Fred. *The Complete Orlando, Florida, Civil Rights Movement: Cooperation, Communication and Recollections 1951–1971.* Cocoa, FL: JAMMIN! Publications 2020.

————. *Recollections of the Orlando, Florida, Civil Rights Movement: A Companion Book to The Orlando Civil Rights Movement: A Case Study in Cooperation and Communication, 1951–1971.* Cocoa, FL: JAMMIN! Publications, 2016.

Bartley, Abel A. *In No Ways Tired: The NAACP's Struggle to Integrate the Duval County Public School System.* Cocoa, FL: Florida Historical Society Press, 2015.

Beeson, Kenneth H., Jr. *Fromajada and Indigo: The Minorcan Colony in Florida.* Charleston, SC: The History Press, 2006.

Branch, Taylor. *Pillar of Fire: America in the King Years, 1963–1965.* New York: Simon & Schuster, 1998.

Brioso, Cesar. *Havana Hardball: Spring Training, Jackie Robinson, and the Cuban League.* Gainesville: University Press of Florida, 2015.

Brotemarkle, Benjamin D. *Crossing Division Street: An Oral History of the African-American Community in Orlando.* Cocoa, FL: Florida Historical Society Press, 2005.

Brown-Smith, Victoria. *Midway-the Midpoint: My Precious Memories of Time Gone By.* New Smyrna Beach, FL: Luther's Publishing, 2002.

Burnett-Haney, C.S. "Florida." In *History of Woman Suffrage Volume IV, 1883–1900,* edited by Ida Husted Harper, 577–80. Indianapolis, IN: Hollenbeck Press.

Bush, Gregory W. *White Sand Black Beach: Civil Rights, Public Space, and Miami's Virginia Key.* Gainesville: University Press of Florida, 2016.

Butler, J. Michael. *Beyond Integration: The Black Freedom Struggle in Escambia County, Florida, 1960–1980.* Chapel Hill: University of North Carolina Press, 2016.

Carlisle, Rodney, and Loretta Carlisle. *Tallahassee in History: A Guide to More Than 100 Sites in Historical Context.* Lanham, MD: Pineapple Press, 2020.

Colburn, David R. *Racial Change & Community Crisis: St. Augustine, Florida 1877–1980.* Gainesville: University of Florida Press, 1991.

Cook-Wilson, Ethel. *Isn't That God's Water? The Advent and Demise of Bethune-Volusia Beach Incorporated.* Self-published, 2015.

Doggett, Carita. *Dr. Andrew Turnbull and the New Smyrna Colony of Florida.* Durham, NC: Light Messages Publishing, 2012.

D'Orso, Michael. *Like Judgement Day: The Ruin and Redemption of a Town Called Rosewood.* New York: Boulevard Books, 1996.

Dunn, Marvin. *Black Miami in the Twentieth Century.* Gainesville: University Press of Florida, 1997.

Evans, Arthur S., and David Lee. *Pearl City, Florida: A Black Community Remembers.* Boca Raton: Florida Atlantic University Press, 1990.

Falkner, David. *Great Time Coming: The Life of Jackie Robinson from Baseball to Birmingham.* New York: Simon & Schuster, 1995.

Green, Ben. *Before His Time: The Untold Story of Harry T. Moore, America's First Civil Rights Martyr.* Gainesville: University Press of Florida, 1999.

Hand, Edie, and Tina Savas. *Women of True Grit: 40 Famous Women Share Real Life Stories with Secrets to Success for All Generations.* Vilas, NC: Canterbury House, 2010.

Hobbs, Tameka Bradley. *Democracy Abroad, Lynching at Home: Racial Violence in Florida.* Gainesville: University Press of Florida, 2015.

Hurst, Jr., Rodney L. *It Was Never About a Hot Dog and a Coke: A Personal Account of the 1960 Sit-In Demonstrations in Jacksonville, Florida and Ax Handle Saturday.* Livermore, CA: WingSpan Press, 2008.

Jones, Maxine D., and Kevin M. McCarthy. *African Americans in Florida.* Sarasota: Pineapple Press, 1993.

Kahrl, Andrew W. *The Land Was Ours: How Black Beaches Became White Wealth in the Coastal South.* Chapel Hill: University of North Carolina Press, 2012.

King, Gilbert. *Devil In the Grove: Thurgood Marshall, the Groveland Boys, and the Dawn of a New America.* New York: Harper-Collins, 2012.

Knighton, Annie Meeks. *Bethune Beach Memoirs: A Pictorial History.* Self-published, 2014.

Kollock, Alice G. "Florida." In *History of Woman Suffrage Volume VI 1900–1920*, edited by Ida Husted Harper, 113–20. Indianapolis, IN: Hollenbeck Press. https://www.gutenberg.org/files/30051/30051-h/30051-h.htm.

Lamb, Chris. *Blackout: The Untold Story of Jackie Robinson's First Spring Training.* Lincoln: University of Nebraska Press, 2004.

Panagopoulos, E.P. *New Smyrna: An Eighteenth Century Greek Odyssey.* Brookline, MA: Holy Cross Orthodox Press, 1978.

Quinn, Jane. *Minorcans in Florida: Their History and Heritage.* St. Augustine, FL: Mission Press, 1975.

Rabby, Glenda Alice. *The Pain and the Promise: The Struggle for Civil Rights in Tallahassee.* Athens: University of Georgia Press, 1999.

Rampersad, Arnold. *Jackie Robinson: A Biography.* New York: Ballantine Books, 1997.

Rasico, Philip D. *The Minorcans of Florida: Their History, Language and Culture.* New Smyrna Beach, FL: Luther's, 1990.

Reider, Franklin. *Can't Get No Satisfaction: A Quest for Racial Equality in Northern Florida in 1965.* Minneapolis: Tasora Books, 2020.

Robertson, Ashley N. *Mary McLeod Bethune in Florida: Bringing Social Justice to the Sunshine State.* Charleston, SC: The History Press, 2015.

Robinson, Jackie, and Alfred Duckett. *I Never Had It Made: The Autobiography of Jackie Robinson.* New York: Ecco Press, reprint 1995.

Robinson, Jackie, and Wendell Smith. *Jackie Robinson: My Own Story.* New York: Greenberg, 1948.

Rymer, Russ. *American Beach: A Saga of Race, Wealth, and Memory.* New York: Harper-Collins, 1998.

Smith, Charles U., ed. *The Civil Rights Movement in Florida and the United States: Historical and Contemporary Perspectives.* Tallahassee: Father & Son, 1989.

Spagna, Ana Maria. *Test Ride on the Sunnyland Bus: A Daughter's Civil Rights Journey.* Lincoln: University of Nebraska Press, 2010.

Vickers, Lu, and Cynthia Wilson-Graham. *Remembering Paradise Park: Tourism and Segregation at Silver Springs.* Gainesville: University Press of Florida, 2015.

Warren, Dan R. *If It Takes All Summer: Martin Luther King, the KKK, and States' Rights in St. Augustine, 1964.* Tuscaloosa: University of Alabama Press, 2008.

Weiss, Elaine. *The Woman's Hour: The Great Fight to Win the Vote.* New York: Penguin Random House, 2918.

Wright, E. Lynn. *More Than Petticoats: Remarkable Florida Women.* Guildford, CT: Morris Book Publishing, 2010.

Young, Andrew. *An Easy Burden: The Civil Rights Movement and the Transformation of America.* New York: Harper Collins, 1996.

Miscellaneous

Baseball Reference. "Jackie Robinson." Accessed September 24, 2022. https://www.baseball-reference.com/players/r/robinja02.shtml.

———. "Johnny Wright." Accessed September 24, 2022. https://www.baseball-reference.com/register/player.fcgi?id=wright007joh.

———. "Lou Rochelli." Accessed September 23, 2022. https://www.baseball-reference.com/players/r/rochelo01.shtml.

———. "Spider Jorgensen." Accessed September 23, 2022. https://www.baseball-reference.com/players/j/jorgesp01.shtml.

Brock, Laura E. "Religion, Sex & Politics: The Story of the Equal Rights Amendment in Florida." Ph.D. diss., Florida State University, 2013.

Center for American Women and Politics. "Teach a Girl to Lead: Women's Suffrage in the U.S. by State." Eagleton Institute of Politics, Rutgers, the State University of New Jersey. Accessed December 20, 2022. https://tag.rutgers.edu/wp-content/uploads/2014/05/suffrage-by-state.pdf.

City of Sanford, Florida. "City Commission Memorandum 20-142 August 10, 2020 Agenda, Resolution No. 2889, Dismissing the Name of the 'Roy G. Williams Park' and restoring the Name of 'Elliott Avenue Park.'" Accessed April 2, 2023. https://media.avcaptureall.com/session.html?sessionid=35dd1552-d44d-47f3-9626-570738f671da.

Civil Rights Library of St. Augustine. "Investigative Report on the Shooting Death of William Kinard." Accessed March 15, 2023. https://civilrights.flagler.edu/digital/collection/p16000coll4/id/1160/.

Evolve Magazines Florida. *The Pride of Florida: Dr. Mary McLeod Bethune's Journey to National Statuary Hall.* 2021.

Florida Memory. "Handwritten Letter from Roxcy Bolton to Thomas V. Zemsta of the Playboy Plaza Hotel, 1971." November 3, 1971. Accessed March 23, 2022. https://www.floridamemory.com/items/show/331458.

———. "Letter from the President of Jordan Marsh Florida to Roxcy Bolton, 1969." Typed letter, September 24, 1969. https://www.floridamemory.com/items/show/331452.

———. "Letter from Vice President and Publicity Director of Burdine's to Roxcy Bolton, 1969." Typed letter, October 13, 1969. https://www.floridamemory.com/items/show/331453.

Grange, Roger, Jr., and Dorothy L. Moore. *Smyrnea Settlement: Archaeology & History of an 18th Century British Plantation in East Florida.* New Smyrna Beach: Southeast Volusia Historical Society. 2016. https://www.nsbhistory.org/smyrnea-settlement/.

League of Women Voters Pensacola Bay Area. *When Women Vote.* 1995; published online 2020. https://www.lwvpba.org/_files/ugd/3332d7_6ef79c64f703473990caeaf5cf146d70.pdf.

Legal Information Institute. "Civil Rights." Cornell Law School. Accessed April 13, 2023. https://www.law.cornell.edu/wex/civil_rights.

Martin Luther King, Jr. Research and Education Institute. "Montgomery Bus Boycott." Stanford University. Accessed August 23, 2022. https://kinginstitute.stanford.edu/encyclopedia/montgomery-bus-boycott.

———. "Supreme Court Affirms Flemming; King States Boycott Will Continue." Stanford University. Accessed August 19, 2022. https://kinginstitute.stanford.edu/encyclopedia/supreme-court-affirms-flemming-king-states-boycott-will-continue.

National Archives. "19th Amendment to the U.S. Constitution: Women's Right to Vote (1920)." Milestone Documents. Accessed December 5, 2022. https://www.archives.gov/milestone-documents/19th-amendment.

Padgett, Gregory B. "C.K. Steele: A Biography." Ph.D. diss., Florida State University, 1994.

Pensacola Journal. Various articles. September 7, 1914. Library of Congress: Chronicling America. Accessed December 6, 2022. https://chroniclingamerica.loc.gov/search/pages/results/?state=&date1=1777&date2=1963&proxtext=pensacola+journal+september+7%2C+1914&x=0&y=0&dateFilterType=yearRange&rows=20&searchType=basic.

Smith, Charles U., and Lewis M. Killian. *Field Reports on Desegregation in the South, Tallahassee, Florida: The Tallahassee Bus Protest.* New York: Anti-Defamation League of B'nai B'rith, 1958.

Stanford Encyclopedia of Philosophy. "Human Rights." Stanford University. Accessed April 13, 2023. https://plato.stanford.edu/entries/rights-human/.

Steele, Charles Kenzie. "The Tallahassee Bus Protest Story." Typescript of speech given on October 26, 1956, at the Florida State Conference of Branches of the National Association for the Advancement of Colored People. Robert and Helen Saunders Papers, series 6, box 50, folder 6. Special Collections Department, University of South Florida, Tampa Campus.

Tallahassee Arts Guide. "Civil Rights Heritage Walk." Accessed August 23, 2022. https://www.tallahasseearts.org/public-art/civil-rights-heritage-walk/.

This Cruel War (blog). "The Anniversary of Duck Hill—A Weekly Look at Historical Lynchings." April 13, 2016. https://thiscruelwar.wordpress.com/2016/04/13/this-disgraceful-evil/.

United States Department of State Office of the Historian. "French and Indian War/Seven Years' War, 1754–63." Milestones: 1750–1775. Accessed December 19, 2022. https://history.state.gov/milestones/1750-1775/french-indian-war.

United States Department of the Interior National Park Service. "City Island Ball Park/Jackie Robinson Ball Park." National Register of Historic Places Nomination Form, 1998.

United States Supreme Court. "*Brown v. Board of Education.*" 1954. Accessed July 15, 2022. https://www.archives.gov/milestone-documents/brown-v-board-of-education#transcript.

University of California, Berkeley. "The 19th Amendment: The Fight for Women's Suffrage as Seen Through 'The Woman Citizen': The 1920 Election." Accessed August 9, 2023. https://exhibits.lib.berkeley.edu/spotlight/women-vote/feature/the-1920-election.

Votapka, Rich. *Fellsmere Firsts*. Revised February 10, 2013. Accessed January 31, 2023. https://www.cityoffellsmere.org/sites/default/files/fileattachments/community_development/page/2151/fellsmere_firsts.pdf.

Wikipedia. "James W. Kynes." Accessed March 15, 2023. https://en.wikipedia.org/wiki/James_W._Kynes.

ABOUT THE AUTHOR

Robert Redd is a native Floridian with a lifelong interest in history. He is a graduate of Stetson University with a BA in American studies and an MA in public history from American Public University. He is a member of the Florida Historical Society, the Southern Historical Association, the American Association of State and Local History and the Civil War Trust, among other local organizations. He is the past executive director of the New Smyrna Museum of History and currently works in the cultural arts field. This marks Roberts's seventh book with Arcadia Publishing. His last two books include *Hidden History of Civil War Florida* and *Florida at Sea: A Maritime History*, coauthored with Nick Wynne and Joe Knetsch. Robert lives in Central Florida with his wife, Christina; dog, Ruby; and cat, Ignatius. He is hard at work on his next book proposal.